Lillian & S... l Cl...
250-4

Lillian & S...... .l Cl......
250-4

GOING HOME

SUBUD MEMBERS' WRITINGS ABOUT DEATH AND DYING

GOING HOME

Compiled and edited by Emmanuel Williams (USA)

Copyright © Emmanuel Williams, USA, July 2014
All rights reserved

No part of this publication may be reproduced, stored in a retrieval system, or transmitted in any form or by any means, electronic, mechanical, photocopying, recording or otherwise without the written permission of the editors.

The views and beliefs presented in this book are exclusively those of the authors and can not be construed as being those of the World Subud Association.

Editorial Assistance: Amelia Williams, Naomi Onaga
Cover Art: © *Ancestors* by Raphaela Riparetti
Layout: Naomi Onaga

"I am swimming in an ocean of love...

I am home"

~ Hamid Camp

INTRODUCTION

Late in 2013 a Subud Palo Alto member, Hamilton Helmer, suggested I work on a collection of Subud members' experiences of death and dying. It seemed like an interesting idea, so I put the word out through the Subud grapevine, sent emails to various poets and writers, and waited. I also collected material by word of mouth: "Got any good stories about death?"

I chose the end of May 2014 as the deadline. I wanted to have the book ready for the Puebla Congress.

It's now July. I keep thinking the book's done – or at least, the "gathering" phase – but people keep sending me more stories, so the door has remained partially open. I'm writing this introduction as a way of drawing a line in the sand. "Enough already!"

The stories and poems are arranged in themed groups. As a 76 year old I'm closer to death than most. Reading these stories and poems has completely erased any fear of death I may have had, and greatly enriched my understanding of a stage that remains for many of us an impenetrable mystery.

I'm very grateful to Emmanuel Elliott, who gave me permission to select stories from his *Reminders of Reality* site.

Thanks to Leonard Lasalle for permission to include two stories from his wonderful book "Source of Life" (available on Lulu.com).

Also I thank Ilaine Lennard for sending me relevant quotes from Bapak's talks.

And my thanks to Doug and Liane Card, Rafiq Dossani, Leanna Harrison, Hamilton Helmer, Danella Maugin, Salamah Pope, Subud Palo Alto, Aminah Ulmer, and Lilliana and Humphrey Williams for their generosity in sponsoring this project.

And to all those whose insights, feelings, and stories are presented on these pages… Thank you, and God bless you. And please forgive me for any mistakes I've made in working on this book.

Emmanuel Williams
July 2014

CONTENTS

The True Life ~ Bapak — 1
REVELATION IN THE DESERT ~ Henrietta Haines — 3

MOTHERS

ACROSS THE GENERATIONS ~ Lillian Truman — 7
REMEMBERING MY MOTHER ~ Hamilton Helmer — 9
AN UNEXPECTED EXPERIENCE ~ Benedict Herrman — 11
…IT IS THE WAY (FOR MOM) ~ Amelia Williams — 13
THE KISS ~ Colin Oliver — 15
WASH YOUR TIRED BODY ~ Rosana Schutte — 16
DANCING IN THE LIGHT ~ Morris McClellan — 17
A LATIHAN EXPERIENCE AT MY MOTHER'S DEATH ~ Anonymous — 19
SPENDING A PENNY ~ Stefan Freedman — 22
TAKING ON THE BURDEN ~ Anonymous — 27
MOTHER'S LOVE ~ Anonymous — 28

A Step Toward Nobility ~ Bapak — 29

FATHERS

FAREWELL TO MY FATHER ~ Anonymous — 33
CONSOLATION FROM AN ANGEL ~ Anonymous — 34
HAPPY HUNTING GROUND ~ Anonymous — 36
MY FATHER'S DEATH ~ Anonymous — 37
LIGHT IN THE KITCHEN ~ Manuela Martinaitis — 39
WHERE HAVE YOU BEEN? ~ Melinda Wallis — 40
WHEE! ~ Michael Thomas — 41
TRAVELLING WITH FATHER ~ Devin Harrison — 43
SAYING GOODBYE ~ Devin Harrison — 44
REQUIEM FOR MY FATHER ~ Irena Olender — 45
ORHAN ~ Liliana Williams — 47
THE OLD KING ~ Emmanuel Williams — 48

The Visitor ~ Bapak — 51

GRANDPARENTS

RITA MAE ~ Arvin Lynes	55
SPARK OF LIFE ~ Hamilton Helmer	57
GOODBYE GG ~ Leonard Lasalle	59
A VISION OF MY GRANDMOTHER ~ Halimah Polk	64
BREATH ~ Harris Smart	65
Illness and Change ~ Bapak	66

SIBLINGS

MY SISTER'S DEATH ~ Harris Boebel	69
SALLY'S PASSING ~ Latifah Taormina	70
THE COLOURS ~ Manuela Martinaitis	74
FOR SUE ~ Malama Macneil	75
THE BREAK ~ FOR ELLA ~ Riantee Rand	77
Three Becoming One ~ Bapak	81

SPOUSES / PARTNERS

DEATH OR BIRTH? ~ Anonymous	85
PEACE ~ Abraham Calman Spivak	86
ON THE DEATH OF MY HUSBAND ~ Latifah Taormina	88
TRANSFORMING FEAR, LOSS OF A SOULMATE ~ Lusijah Rott	89
REMEMBERING RAMDHAN ~ Mardiyah Simpson	95
FAREWELL TO A MARINER ~ Mardiyah Simpson	99
An Opener of the Way ~ Bapak	101

FRIENDS

A FRIEND'S SUICIDE ~ Anonymous	
NO SMELL OF COFFEE ~ Laurie Lathrop	106

LOOKING AT THE OCEAN ~ Manuel Oliver	108
MY FRIEND JO ~ Adrienne Thomas	109
REMEMBERING RIDWAN ~ Lilliana Gibbs	111
UNANSWERED QUESTION ~ Stephanie Ferreira	113
ANIMAL SIGHTINGS ~ Elna Kelly	114
COLORED LIGHTS ~ Reynold Weissinger	115

Ready to Go ~ Bapak   117

ANCESTORS

REMEMBERING OUR FOREBEARS ~ Leonard Hitchcock	121
BLUE AND RED ROADS ~ Anonymous	123

CHILDREN

DELIVERANCE ~ Rasunah Katz	129
SANDY HOOK ~ Emmanuel Williams	131
AIDS ~ Chellie Kew	133
TAKING MY BABY TO HEAVEN ~ Amelia Williams	134

MULTIPLES

DANELLA'S STORY ~ Danella Mauguin	137
HANIA'S STORY ~ Hani'a Hummingbird Hototo	139
DYING BY DEGREES ~ Kadarijah Gardiner	142
KADARIJAH'S 100TH DAY ~ Sharifin Gardiner	144
THE DEATH OF RACHMAN ULMER ~ Aminah Herrman, family and a friend	145

Life in Death ~ Bapak   159

SADNESS

UNEXPECTED WINTER ~ Miranda Hampton	163
GRIEF ~ Ilona Merlin	164

NATURE OF DEATH

ON DEATH AND DYING ~ Salamah Pope	167
WHAT IT IS ALL ABOUT ~ Daphne Tibbs	171
AWAKENING ~ Nuraini Magnusson	172
GATES OF WINTER ~ Theresa Whitehill	174
WHAT HAPPENED TO ME ONCE ~ Mardiyah Tarantino	175
The Jiwa's Own Life ~ Bapak	177

ANGELS

OTHER LIVES ~ Anonymous	181
THE TRAGEDY OF 11 SEPTEMBER 2001 ~ Leonard Lasalle	183
Jesus and the Angel Doctor ~ Bapak	185

MESSAGES FROM BEYOND

RAINDROPS ARE FALLING ON MY HEAD ~ Anonymous	189
A VISIT FROM VARINDRA ~ Anonymous	190
MESSAGE FROM ELSIE ~ Manuel Oliver	191
MY COUSIN'S DEATH ~ Anonymous	192
BEING RABIN ~ Anonymous	194
I WAS THERE ~ Anonymous	195
The Symbolism of the Crucifixion ~ Bapak	197

SPIRITS

LEAVING THE APARTMENT ~ Shoshana Margolin	201
GRAVEYARD SHIFT ~ Anonymous	202
Ghosts and the material force ~ Bapak	203

AT THE GATES

DIALOGUE ~ Illia Thompson	207
ST PETER AT THE GATE ~ Theresa Whitehill	209

NEAR DEATH EXPERIENCES / COMING BACK FROM THE DEAD

MY SECRET ~ Anonymous	213
THE LAKE ~ Leonard Hitchcock	214
I DIED WHEN I WAS 16, BUT HERE I AM ~ Ra'ue Ramsey	215
SURVIVING A CAR CRASH ~ Anonymous	217
THE SIGN ~ Anonymous	218
A new experience for Bapak ~ Bapak	219

PREPARATIONS

IN DEATH ~ Halimah Polk	223
MR SANDS ~ Ann Padilla	227
DRIVER TRAINING ~ Amelia Williams	229
MY SENSES OF MY OWN DEATH ~ Theodore Salisbury	230
REST EASY ~ Cesca Wright	233
THE CALL HOME ~ Serafina	234
LAST WISHES ~ Malama MacNeil	236
Why the Latihan is Needed ~ Bapak	239
I AM HOME ~ Paul Edwards	241
An Overnight Stop ~ Bapak	243

The True Life

In reality, when you die it's not like a bird flying away from its cage. No. If you have reached what you need for your individuality, what you need for your human soul, then it is like night following day, like day following night.

The question is: what happens after you die? Bapak describes it like this. This is your life now ~ then after you are dead it goes on but it's different. Before, it was like this, then all at once you die ~ you're dead ~ then you're like this again but not the same. (Bapak demonstrates, opening and closing his eyes. Laughter.) The way you open your eyes will not be like this, it will be with your seeing.

That is why Bapak always says to just continue the latihan, because in the latihan little by little all the windows are opened. What windows is Bapak talking about? The window of the eyes is opened, the window of the ears is opened, the window of the nose is opened, the window of the mouth is opened, the window of the heart is opened, the window of the brain is opened ~ all the windows are opened. They begin to be opened... opened... opened..., and then you realize:

'Oh, so this is life after death, the true life'...

> Bapak
> Chicago, Illinois U.S.A.
> June 23, 1959

REVELATION IN THE DESERT

~ HENRIETTA HAINES

Back in 1989 a friend of mine, whom some of you may remember – Lucilla Warren – had invested a lot of energy into believing the story of the 11:11, a much publicized magical event that was billed as the day and the hour of immense worldwide Enlightenment.

I personally received that this was pretty much a scam to sell the book that sold the idea. However, it seemed ungenerous and unkind not to support such an old friend. So about a dozen of us piled into cars and headed out from the Westside of LA to the Mojave Desert to await the great revelation.

As luck would have it, by the time we got there it was late and cold, I was dead tired and grouchiness was overtaking me. So I took my grouchy self, laid it down on the ground and went to sleep. Lucilla promised she would wake the sleepers in time to get in the proper receptive frame of mind for the divine moment.

She woke me with only minutes to spare. I found a spot of dirt in Mojave's vastness that seemed propitious enough for enlightenment and sat on it. During that time I had been worrying about what I was supposed to accomplish here on earth before I died. Death wasn't impending, but I thought if I was going to do anything complicated I better get on with whatever preparation might be needed. I prayed to know what that great something was or at least what preparation I should start on.

Then I got quiet and in a flash I heard this message about my birth, my life and my death.

"Henrietta… Life is like a trip to Paris. You go. You have a nice lunch with friends and then you come home."

That was it. The whole message, the whole deal.

I am grateful for my revelation.

It's only lunch Henrietta, only lunch. Then come home.

MOTHERS

ACROSS THE GENERATIONS

~ LILLIAN TRUMAN

We all have bereavements, but the road can be as lonely as life itself can be, and different for each one of us. It seems that God is the only constant, and I guess that has to be enough, but sometimes, I know, He can seem far away.

My mother told me that she couldn't believe in God, though she had tried. I and my husband were in Subud and mum lived with us and our 2 small children. She was bedridden and very deaf–this was all 23 years ago. Anyway, I felt that I wanted her so much to be in Subud, but felt it to be very wrong to open her as she had no real concept of Subud and had not asked.

After long coma, Mum died, and I was close by her bed. Thinking I could do much for mum in prayer now (especially as I was in Subud), I fell to my knees and was going to pray when I kind of heard a voice say very clearly that my mother had no need of my prayers. That was very humbling. I realise that I had been feeling a kind of one-upmanship because of Subud. Then the house seemed full of light and I was given for many days grace of quiet and peace. I thought it would last forever, and was bereft when it left me. Who knows why graces are taken and given?

About a year or so ago, my daughter Ruth, who lives in London and is in Subud, went to a Subud Congress. She phoned us one evening to tell us that she had just opened my mother. From the way she told us about it we knew that it had truly happened.

Up to that time Ruth had never shown much interest in my mom. Ruth was only 2 years old when mum died, and though I talked of my mother, it was hard for my daughters to be really that interested – youth looks to youth, I think.

At the Congress Ruth had mentioned to helpers that she felt heavy, as though there was literally a burden on her shoulders. Helpers tested around the burden for quite a while until they found that it was my mother with Ruth. One helper asked mum if she wanted to be opened, but could not even finish the question because the answer was so sure, my mother light and helpers feeling her hugging them. There followed a wonderfully light latihan for all.

Ruth says she often feels my mum around her and in latihan – very light and loving.

At about this time the then regional helper, Melinda Lasalle, visited our group on the island. She spoke with me about her own daughter opening her grandmother. Melinda was so very glad that her mother-in-law was free somehow. Melinda also explained that we very often latihan for our ancestors, men for men ancestors and women for women ancestors. She also said that it seems that parents skip a generation, and are helped not by their children, but by their grandchildren, or rather, the grandchild they feel closest to.

This is all too much, frankly, for my head, but if I can just feel, then it feels good. I also feel that failing Subud, and multitudes are not in Subud, then God finds other ways for all to help each other, in death as in life. More than that I can't even guess at.

For myself, I feel my mother close in music. She so loved much music, and when I hear something I know she would have loved then she seems very near. Here is a poem by Siegfried Sassoon that you may like to have.

When I'm alone

I thought of age, and loneliness, and change.
I thought how strange we grow when we're alone,
and how unlike the cells that meets, and talk,
then blow the candles out, and say good night.
Alone... The word is life endured and known.
It is the stillness where our spirits walk
and all but inmost faith is overthrown.

I send this with love in Subud.

April 4th 1994

REMEMBERING MY MOTHER

~ HAMILTON HELMER

Mom was my mother, my friend, my spiritual mentor and my unflagging champion.

My memories are rich in recollections of her constant gift of love: happy summer days swimming at Silver Lake, school lunch picnics in the spring grass of May, a letter every day for four years when I was at boarding school, a cross-continent pilgrimage with Dad to see Bapak, excursions to the latest movie with dinner before, Easter visits to Aunt Ruth's, lunches with Gram at the Long Trail Lodge, happy Christmas' every year in Woodstock, Indian Summer days in England after Dad's death, a phone call in the last week of her life just to tell me how much she loved me. It's endless. A few weeks before her death I gave Mom a book with the inscription: "You were always there when I needed you". This is what I felt – unquestioning love and support. We quibbled about the little things – never the big things.

Mom's life was not always easy. She was shocked into adulthood when, in a brief span in her youth, a drunken driver, a German torpedo and a heart attack suddenly robbed her of her only two brothers and her father. But Mom did not retreat, instead she exuberantly embraced life.

God was the epicenter of Mom's life. Her greatest gift to me was the example of an unwavering commitment to God and doing His work. Material things, success, the opinions of others were unimportant in the face of God. We were here to discover and carry out His Will – it's that simple and that hard. This understanding has enriched every element of my life: my marriage, my children, my work, my worship. Some month's ago I had a dream that I was standing in the transept of the church in Orwell that her mother and father frequented. I was overcome by a transcending inner warmth, flooded with a thankfulness to the many generations of my ancestors that had led straightforward, God-fearing lives. Their devotion and sacrifices are the foundation on which I stand. Mom was an unfaltering link in this great chain.

When someone you love dies, you are always touched in two very different ways: how you feel and your sense of how they are. For me, I am sad. I will miss the frequent calls on my cell phone, the reminders to take my vitamins, the queries about the latest movies, the back and forth about the stock market, Bart's latest adventures. I find myself reaching for the phone only to withdraw my hand, realizing no one will be there to answer. I resent the prospect of someone I love being replaced by ever fading memories. There is a hole in my heart that time's weeds may cover but never heal. But that's the price life exacts for love.

For Mom though I have no worries. She is in a better place. Earlier this year I dreamt she would die, so I knew it was coming and had prepared my family. It was time for her. She had finished her business here, and she needed to move on. She had nurtured and protected two loving sons. She had been a devoted and adored wife. She had heeded her Muse, leaving a wealth of soul-centered poems. She had secured us financially. She had seen six wonderful grandchildren transform from the malleable clay of infancy into vibrant human beings. She had seen us through good times and hard times. Her duty done, her example followed and her love evident, the next life called. She had but one final lesson to leave us: how to speed the journey to God's kingdom by gracefully surrendering to God with dignity and resolve. Her example of a cheerful and life-filled final journey is indelibly etched into my being. It was her finest hour. Her first legacy to me was how to embrace life, while never losing touch with God. Her final legacy was just as significant: how to sense the subtle scent of the ebb of life's call and effortlessly succumb to God's beckoning.

On several occasions, Mom recounted to me a powerful dream she had had many years ago. Death came to her. Ominous, numinous, wrapped in black robes, Death said "It is time, but I can grant you one last wish before you come with me." Mom paused not a heartbeat, and said "All I want is a day in June". She was instantly transported. The sun shone with its equinal warmth, the grass was the rich green of an early Vermont summer, the wildflowers bloomed in profuse, multi-colored splendor, insects were humming and the vibrant expectancy of youth filled the air. She looked around, inhaled deeply and took it all in. She was full of life but also full of peace. She turned to death, who was still at her side, and said "I'm ready now, take me to where I must go." Death replied "You are already there."

I love you Mom. I'll miss you. Thank you for everything. Goodbye and God's speed.

AN UNEXPECTED EXPERIENCE

~ BENEDICT HERRMAN

My mother had been an alcoholic, but was devoted to my father, who had died about a year and a half before she passed. She had undergone surgery for a small spot of colon cancer, which the doctors had successfully removed, but her liver was so far gone from cirrhosis that she was unable to process the anesthesia out of her system. I visited her in the hospital, but she soon slipped into a coma as her battered system slowly shut down. I came every so often to check on her, and swab out her mouth with little lemon swabs the hospital had by her bedside to keep her from getting too dry. She could not communicate. I asked a couple of women helpers to open her, but they tested and felt that wasn't her path. A month passed.

One morning at about 6:00 AM, I got a call from her doctor saying that I had better get there soon. I went over, and entered her room, but she had just passed momentarily before. I felt very quiet and light, and not wracked with grief, as I thought I might be. As I stood next to her body, contemplating the woman who had born and raised me, I began to feel a light, joyous energy floating somewhere in the room. It appeared to come from a single area, up near the ceiling where the wall joins it. I continued being quiet, and somehow felt it was my mother AND father, together again, and the happiness in the room was palpable. My sorrow was non-existent; instead my heart was glad she was not suffering, and felt joy in her new state, and her re-connection with my father.

The chaplain came in and tried to 'comfort' me, though I was not in need of it. I let him pray, and could hardly wait for him to leave so I could be alone to sense the joy floating in the room above me. He finally left, and in a while I decided to go home, as there was nothing more I could do in the hospital.

As I drove home, this joyous, loving feeling followed me, and as I entered the house, the energy I had felt before again settled into a particular area where the wall and ceiling met. This energy then 'followed' me around the house for about 4 hours. I slowly realized they were checking on me, concerned for me. I turned to it and looked up at where I felt it to be and said, "I'm alright. Thank you for being wonderful, loving parents, and thank you for everything you did for me. I love you both. Please… go where you need to go next. I'm fine."

As if on cue, the energy vanished, and I was alone again, at home, feeling grateful to God for the unexpected experience that proved to me that death is just a doorway out of this plane, and into another.

•

... IT IS THE WAY (FOR MOM)

~ AMELIA WILLIAMS

When your impending monument
Lifted by eons of structural rearrangement
Finally cracks and crumbles
Edifice avalanching to depths and plateaus
Carried on watery caravans
To reach tide-lined destiny
. . . I do not fear
The loss of grounding
But revel in your
Transformation and arrival
As you join and in-fill
Stretch of sand across shore.
   . . . It is the way.

When your ice palace
Hailing from lofty cloud space
Softens its hold of self on self
Slips and slides from heights
Rushing to travel the path
Or forge new routes
Screaming, tumbling, calming, drifting
Winding towards ultimate fusion
In shock of wave-splash
. . . I do not weep
The loss of your royal vista
But marvel the vast fury
Of your sea-fullness.
   . . . It is the way.

When your breath inflates
To breeze, then gust
Ripping across expanses
Leveling neglect, regret and hope
Until the hush returns
. . . I do not cling
To landscapes and memories
But embrace your democratic erasure
Promising a new beginning.
    . . . It is the way.

When your life began to falter
Built upon a foundation of
Hopes and disappointments
Asking and doubting
Knowing and not knowing
Of echoes and dreams
When your heart floated
Into certainty of love
Radiant, and embraced by light
And your life slipped silently
To the other side
When you passed through fires
Transmuting the last residual
Hold on doubt and encumbrance
When you soared to a new life of
Warmth, safety and knowing
. . . I did not grieve
But shed tears celebrating the witness
Of your extraordinary journey
Your persistent reach for undeniable truth
Your arrival at a destiny
You dared not dream existed.
    . . . You found your way.
    . . . I love you.

THE KISS

~ COLIN OLIVER

She comes in a dream.
She comes to retrieve
her final days,
the bruised frailty,
and set in their place
another time. I stand
before her in the scuffed light
of a station, the end of
a visit, her daughter
newly beside me.
She wears a summer dress.
Her goodbye
is a deft kiss. In the pool
of memory
it switches down
like a silver coin. I wake
from the dream to the first
hint of morning. Remember
the kiss, she says.

WASH YOUR TIRED BODY

~ ROSANA SCHUTTE

Give me death, love.
Give me death of a heart
to widen the space.
O Hand Divine
show me mercy,
your special brand of Grace

Widen me, deepen me
an ocean for my fellows.
A sea of love,
drift in me, be still in me.
Wash your tired body.

Give me death, love.
Give me death of a heart
White orchids waft the air
to widen the space.
O Hand Divine
show me mercy,
your special brand of Grace

O Adored, come to shore
strip free of mortal woes.
A nurture deep
plunge in me, play in me.
Wash your tired body.

From living waters, rising anew
I am your child.
I am your bride.

Dear Sweet Life, breathe last breath
upon my thirsty lips.
Eternal kiss.
Taste of soft lavender.

I'll give you death love.
I'll give you death of a heart
to widen the space.
O Child Divine,
receive mercy.
Belovéd, be loved by me.

July 22, 2002

DANCING IN THE LIGHT

~ MORRIS MCCLELLAN

Up in the attic, hot and dusty, it smelled of dry, unfinished wood,
I found my grandad's keepsakes, from his days of parenthood.
There were letters from a daughter who had married and
 moved away,
Reports on life's grand adventures, and a child was on the way.
Of the photos she had sent him he had framed one for his room,
Taken by her husband on a hillside all in bloom.
The sun shown down so brightly on a day when all was right
Her beauty filled that meadow, as she danced there in the light.

Chorus:
    She was dancing in the light, she was dancing in the light
    Her eyes were shining upward, she was taken by delight
    And the flowers she had tossed were at the apex of their flight
    When my father's snapshot caught my momma,
        Dancing in the Light

To see my mother young and vital, in the fullness of her prime
I seemed to lose my grip somehow, I stepped outside of time
How long has she been gone now? But my heartaches still remain
Since the year that I lost my momma, I have never been the same
But now this photo in its frame has caused my sadness to be still
I don't know how it's done it, perhaps I never will
All the pictures I have of her I value more than gold
Oh but this one I will cherish, yes, this one I will hold

Chorus:
    She was dancing in the light, she was dancing in the light
    Her eyes were shining upward, she was taken by delight
    And the flowers she had tossed were at the apex of their flight

When my father's snapshot caught my momma,
   Dancing in the Light

   Bridge:

   I hear my mother's voice, she says it's best to let her go
   But see her now, as God can see her,
   She thought I'd want to know
   She thought I'd want to know, that she was…

She was dancing in the light, she was dancing in the light
Her eyes were shining upward, she was taken by delight
Her soul had its own journey as she tried to do things right
When my father's snapshot caught my momma,
   Dancing in the Light

She was dancing in the light, she was dancing in the light
Her eyes were shining upward, she was taken by delight
And the flowers she had tossed were at the apex of their flight
When my father's snapshot caught my momma, Dancing in the Light

© 2000 by Myckle Mirth Music, BMI

A LATIHAN EXPERIENCE AT MY MOTHER'S DEATH

~ ANONYMOUS

In his book *Susila Budhi Dharma*, Bapak writes that if a person does their latihan sincerely "their progress will benefit their parents, whether they wish it or not." He adds: "It can be said that the child may be able to raise their parents to a higher level," and "Even if it is not your intention to correct your parents' faults their inner content will be spontaneously influenced."

When I read this, I hoped it might be possible one day, but didn't see how it could really happen in my own difficult family circumstances.

Because of these I left home when I was only 18 and joined Subud at once, hoping it would help me to feel better and that I might be able to live a more sensible and stable life than my parents had done. Neither my father nor my mother was interested in joining so at that time I was the only member of my family in Subud. Back then if you were under 21 you had to get a signed letter from your parents giving you permission to join, which they gave only when they heard men and women did latihan separately!

My mother was an orphan who had been brought up by Spiritualists who practiced table-turning to summon the dead, which terrified her; she was afraid that Subud would be the same as this. Although I explained to her that Subud was not like Spiritualism, I understood her fears and just carried on with my own latihan regardless. However, after seven years I married a Subud member and soon afterwards my mother had a strange experience.

My husband and I visited her on the way back from a large Subud congress where I had received the most powerful latihan I had ever experienced. When we met my mother, she told us that she'd been woken in the night by three Malaysian-looking ladies wearing sarongs who told her it was now time for her to be opened in Subud. (My mother had lived in Malaya and recognised their clothing, which is similar to that worn by Indonesians).

According to my mother, the room became filled with vivid colour, even though the light was off, and she then saw me floating near the ceiling, advising her not to be scared but just to surrender to God. She said it was not a dream.

This experience frightened her even more as afterwards she said she felt a very strong vibration which would not stop and she asked me to turn it off! I didn't know what to do about this so reported it to the local Subud group who asked her to come along and be properly opened. She refused, so I wrote to Sudarto Martohudojo (Bapak's helper) about her experience and he too advised she should be opened, but still she refused. Sudarto advised me not to force her to do anything.

Later, my mother developed serious mental health problems and Parkinson's disease and became severely depressed. Her life with my father had involved her in many dangerous life-threatening situations which led to our family becoming refugees in three different war zones and there were other stresses in the marriage which had taken their toll on her over the years. Nevertheless, uncharacteristically, my father became her sole carer, refusing all help offered to him by his children and by the local authorities and charities. Still, he looked after her to the best of his ability and towards the end of her life held private prayer sessions with her, enjoining her to pray to Jesus for help and peace.

This went on for two years, with my mother steadily deteriorating until she finally committed suicide.

Of course I was devastated and as we drove to the funeral I felt even worse, and didn't know how I'd get through it. I was particularly sad because although I hadn't really expected the latihan to touch my parents' souls in the way Bapak described in his book, I never dreamt that she'd actually deteriorate to the stage of killing herself.

As we drew nearer to the church where the funeral was to be held I suddenly had such a strong spontaneous experience that I asked my husband who was driving to stop the car. Even though I thought we might be too late to attend the service I just couldn't bear to go any further. I was fully aware of sitting in the front seat next to my husband when all at once I felt my soul being lifted up out of my body and then I could see myself from high above, still in the car seat. I was pulled up higher and higher and then I suddenly found myself in a church filled with light. I saw that on either side of the church people were sitting in pews and they were all wearing white robes. I was then told they were my ancestors and they were dressed in white to signify they were dead and that they had come to witness the ceremony.

I then realised that leaning on my arm was my mother, looking very ill indeed, and on her other side was my father who supported her with his arm. She had to be propped up by both of us as we slowly proceeded down the central aisle of the church towards the altar. There at the end of the aisle stood a radiant figure that I knew was Jesus. His face was so bright I couldn't look at it; from his heart shone rays of light and warmth and love. When we reached him he gave my mother Holy Communion from a communion chalice and then a door opened which she went through alone. She had been accepted.

I was then told this was Heaven where I would go when I died and was asked if I would like to stay there now? This horrified me as I had three small children at the time and begged to be allowed to return to them. Then I was told I could go back to my life on Earth and having made this decision was told I would live until I was at least 63 after which my work in this world would be completed and I could then live on as long as was granted. Afterwards I returned to my body safely and we were able to get to the funeral on time; all the time I was fully conscious of simultaneously still sitting in the car seat.

This whole experience resulted in my faith in God being strengthened and my belief in Bapak's words that a person's latihan can affect the state of their parents' souls. It also happened that later on I was asked to work in a psychiatric hospital as an art therapist with patients who had tried to commit suicide. It was my job to try to help them to find happiness in life on their journey towards recovery and rehabilitation. I enjoyed this work so much I continued it for twelve years until my retirement.

I hope that if anyone reading this has also experienced the pain of suicide in their family that this article might help them.

From *Reminders of Reality*

SPENDING A PENNY
(DEDICATED TO THE VENERABLE CLUB I'LL SOON BE JOINING)

~ STEFAN FREEDMAN

What time is it?
3.30
Ron's taking forever, isn't he?
No mum, he's only been gone a moment
Do you think he's all right?
Of course?
Are you sure?
Please don't worry, mum.
Well would you just phone and ask if he's OK
But he's only called round next door. He'll just be having a little chat.
So you think he's all right?
Yes.
But I wonder what's keeping him so long.
Mom, as soon as someone leaves the room you start worrying.
Do I really dear?
Everything's fine. Really.
What time is it now?
3.31
Did you hear that funny noise?
What kind of noise?
Like someone trying to break in by the back door.
No.
Dear, just go and check, would you, that no one's out in the garden.
OK. Just to reassure you.
Don't be long.
Don't worry, mum
Dora, DORA! Is there somebody out there?
I don't know. I'm not there yet.
WAIT! COME BACK NOW DORA. QUICK I NEED YOU NOW.
I'm right here, mum, here I am. Are you all right?

What time is it?
3.32
Don't go out there. I don't want you going out. He could become violent.
Who?
Just stay here, close to me.
It's OK, I'm staying with you, mum.
What are we going to do about that violent man outside?
But I didn't hear or see anyone.
Am I the only one in this house who notices things?
You never miss a trick, mum.
Don't you think Ron is taking too long? What on earth can he possibly be doing?
Chatting. He's not been 5 minutes. Please don't worry.
What time is it?
3.33. And look, see? He's coming back. I'm going to the loo now.
The what?
The toilet.
You know I find that word crass, dear. We always call it "spending a penny".
Hi Ron, mum was worried about you. OK I'm just going to "spend a penny". I suppose that must be worth about one pee!
Dora! Don't be vulgar.
Only joshing, mum.
When you're incontinent, there's nothing entertaining about that subject!
Sorry mum.
Ron, I see that you prefer the neighbours, don't you! That's why you deserted us. Will you have a nice cup of tea, dear?
That'd be lovely
Put the kettle on then, Ron, and make me one too, while you're at it.
Righty-ho, Mrs Radcliffe
Don't you think Dora's looking ill?
She seems in fine form to me.
What have you been doing to her? She looks pale and exhausted.
I hadn't noticed.
Am I the only one who notices things? What time is it?
3.34
Why is Dora taking so long?
She's been gone all of twenty seconds!

Do you think she's all right?
She's spent a penny on several past occasions and survived.
Don't cheek me! I need you to check, dear.
Have you noticed, the minute someone leaves the room, you start to worry?
Just knock on the door to make sure she's OK. And for heaven's sake put the kettle on will you?
Dora's fine, Mrs Radcliffe, honestly.
You don't know. She could be unconscious.
She's fine, I promise!
Or dead.
What makes you say that?
It can happen. I just heard it on the news. A man was found dead while spending a penny.
That was a starving Albanian stowing away on a train in Italy.
You see? These things do happen. It can happen to anyone, anywhere.
OK OK! (calling) Dora, are you still alive?
NO! I'M DEAD AND THIS IS MY GHOST TALKING. WHOOOO!
I think your daughter's going bonkers Mrs Radcliffe but she's still mortal. See?
What's the time?
3.35
Don't you think she's taking a terribly long time?
I'll go and put the kettle on, now.
Come straight back.
Mum? Would you like a nice cup of tea?
I begged Ron for one ages ago but he never listens to me.
I bet he's making it right now.
What's the time?
3.36
Don't you think Ron's taking an awfully long time?
No. You're always anxious about time, mum.
Am I? What is the time, dear?
Look I've brought you those handmade chocolates you loved last visit. Went specially to Lavenham to get them for you.
This box is very small compared to the last one.
Actually it's identical.
You think I'm so old and stupid I won't notice?
You notice everything, mum, but honestly it's identical to the ones you enjoyed

last time.
Nora gets me something different every visit. Not just the same thing repeatedly.
I love you Mum and…
What time is it now?
Look mum…
Where has my tea gone to?
Here Mrs Radcliffe. I'm right here. Kettle took a minute to boil. I opened up these Jaffa cakes, would you like one with your tea?
But there was a packet of digestives already open. Didn't you see them?
Where?
In the tin in the top cupboard behind the prunes. Why didn't you look there first?
Oh dear, Mrs Radcliffe, I stand corrected. I've been a naughty boy again!
What time is it?
3.37
Isn't it time you two were going?
What? But we came all this way just to spend this afternoon with you, mum.
Well since you arrived you both haven't stopped dashing in and out. It makes me deeply anxious you know.
What does?
That my family don't take proper care of me. Noone loves or supports me.
Mum, that's why we're here!
Yes, but you visit only because you can't bear the thought of me coming down to live with you.
Mom, how many times have we talked all this through? There's the steep staircase and we truly don't have any space.
Yes I see, dear! Ron, you've no idea how it pains me to see the very child who I brought into this world abandoning me. I'm devastated and it's so unfair. All my friends agree that she's cold and heartless. Years of mothering and you get thrown out like an old sofa! It makes me bitterly ashamed of my own family.
I'm sorry to see you unhappy, mum. We love you, mum. Look! While we're here is there anything at all we can do for you?
There's always plenty that needs doing, but don't you go bothering yourselves!
Ah dear, mum…
What time is it?
3.38
Did I tell you, I'm changing my will.

Why's that?
You know perfectly well. You're the only one that doesn't see what your real problem is?
My upbringing?
Don't be silly! I'm deadly serious
OK, tell me.
I need you to heed me for once.
OK, tell me, mum, I'm listening.
You never think of a living soul besides yourself!

TAKING ON THE BURDENS

~ ANONYMOUS

My mother died shortly after my 16th birthday. I missed her a lot, but also knew I had to get on with life, and I prayed for her. When I was 28 years old I was opened in Subud. I had only been doing the latihan for a few months when I had an interesting experience. I was at home and my husband, two children, and the dog were getting into the car for a trip to see my father in my old family home. My father had decided to sell up and live with his sister, and the whole of my family (I have three brothers) were getting together to share out the knick knacks and unwanted furniture from the house. It was an important family occasion as we were also saying goodbye to the house in which we had all been brought up. As I was getting in the car I realised that I had forgotten something and dashed back into the house to fetch it from the upstairs bedroom while everyone else waited in the car. When I came out to the upstairs landing, my mother was suddenly and unexpectedly "there," about six feet off the ground. It was a wonderful shock, because I had never felt her presence since she died. I "spoke" to her and explained what I was doing. I then heard myself say "It's alright, I'll take over from here". I had no idea what I meant(!!), but I knew it was something important about unfinished business, and I guessed it was about reconciling her relationship with my father, which had been very poor when she was alive. Later I was recounting this to one of the group helpers, and she asked how old my mother would have been had she lived. I said 63 years old. I didn't know at the time that Bapak had said that at 63, much of your "nafsu" is passed on to your offspring ..... everything fell into place then, and I carried the burden with joy knowing I was helping my mother as well as myself.

From *Reminders of Reality*

MOTHER'S LOVE

~ ANONYMOUS

My relationship with my mother had not been very loving or supportive, but it improved after I joined Subud, and especially after my daughters were born. I saw changes and an inner softening taking place in her. After my father died, she visited me in California and came to sit outside the latihan.

As it turned out she didn't ask to be opened at that time. About 20 years later, some months prior to her death, she was going in for emergency surgery 3,000 miles away, and there was the possibility that she wouldn't make it. She agreed over the phone for 'special prayers' to be done for her at a specific time and I asked several Subud helpers to gather with me and do a latihan for her. We received to open her at a distance. Four months later I went to be with her as she was dying. I would sing to her as she slept and once sang Ibu Sumari's prayer which always brings great peace. However, after my mother's death I was once again feeling that she never loved me. I was doing latihan and testing with two Subud helpers and one of them was getting the sense that I was angry and asking, "Why didn't you tell me you loved me all these years?" So I asked, "What can I do to heal this anger and emotional pain?" I received a powerful worship and an awareness of surrendering it all to God, albeit in a rather demanding way. It was as if I was saying to God, "That isn't enough, I need to know if mother loved me." Then my latihan completely changed: it was as if the ceiling of the living room opened up and I saw my mother lounging on a cloud looking down at me. She looked about 23 years old, so happy and free without any cares or worries. She smiled at me and said, "My sweet dear, I'm so sorry, I do love you and I'm so proud of you and what you gave to me," and she looked around at her heavenly surroundings. "I couldn't have come here without your help, I was so stuck." Then I saw myself as a newborn through her eyes, and then as a little girl "a child of grace so sweet."

And she said, "I was so caught up in my own difficulties – jealousy, frustrations and problems from my own childhood. I do love you so very much." And I saw myself with my arms up to God as though my mother's love was like an armload of ethereal air flowers raining down on me and this lasted several minutes. Then the 'window' closed up and became a ceiling again and I felt so deeply blessed, healed and at peace with my mother.

From *Reminders of Reality*

A Step Toward Nobility

...there is no creature in this world that does not fear death. For death comes only once to all creatures.

Once it has come, that's it, it is finished, and all creatures must die. So therefore, this is not a small thing if you are able to find the conviction and the strength of mind and the firm faith which can take you through this barrier. And you will then understand that exactly as the messengers of God have always said in the past that man is created to live both in this life and in the next life. That life goes on and life is something continuous. The only difference is that here man lives in the vehicle of his coarse body. Whereas there, man lives in the vehicle of his pure or holy feeling. But the life is still the same.

In other words, that death is not something to be afraid of, but a step up for man towards nobility. And all this is something that we receive, the reality of this we receive in the latihan kejiwaan. For the messengers of God have told us that life is continuous, and therefore we do not need to worry about death.

Only while in this life we must act rightly. We must not do something, which is of the nature of hurting other people, or reducing other people's happiness, or reducing other people's security and welfare, or of making other people sad.

In other words, we must live in harmony in this life.

> Bapak
> Toronto, Canada
> May 17, 1976

FATHERS

FAREWELL TO MY FATHER

~ ANONYMOUS

My father and I hadn't been very close. He had a business to run and was always away working. Children tend to be self-centred and I was resentful of him never being at home and giving me any attention. Later when I grew up I realised that my father simply didn't have the time or energy to spend much time with his children because he was working very hard to sustain his family. I was able to forgive him and instead wished that I had been of more help to him.

Around the time my father died I had been particularly resentful of him. I was a 13 year old boy and it was towards the end of the summer holiday. Most of my friends had done things together with their fathers: some went on fishing trips, others went to football matches or did other activities together, while I hardly ever saw my dad.

The day my father died I woke up around 8 am. I went downstairs to make myself breakfast. I noticed that the atmosphere in the house was different. The weather had been particularly bad that week, there had been a lot of noise around the house because of the rain and wind and the night before there had been a storm, but now everything was still and peaceful. When I passed the sitting room I could see my father sleeping on the sofa. He was still wearing his suit and tie, but he sometimes came home late from work and fell asleep on the sofa so this was not unusual. Something made me stop and watch him this time however. There was something angelic about his face, the way he lay there sleeping.

A ray of sunshine entered through the window and lit the room. This, together with the strange quietness and peacefulness that was in the house had the effect on me that I felt my eyes filled with tears and I wanted to weep. A feeling of forgiveness and love arose in me towards my father. He then woke up, and instead of avoiding his company and being critical and resentful towards him, as had been my habit for years, I was moved to help him and I asked him if he needed anything. We spent about 20 minutes together with a lovely warm feeling between us, though all the time I was fighting back the tears.

My father went to work and later in the afternoon a phone call came telling us that he had collapsed and had died of a heart attack. I am forever grateful that I was able to part with him in this way on the day he died.

From *Reminders of Reality*

CONSOLATION FROM AN ANGEL

~ ANONYMOUS

It was the day after my father's passing. Through my latihan, over a period of half a year, I had gone through a process of preparation for this event: I had seen that it was God's will for my father to die, I had been trained to keep my emotions out of this process of preparing for death, I had gone through my own mourning and so I was able to experience the day of his passing and the weeks to follow in a state of quiet bliss and gratefulness for being able to be a witness to this process of a beloved one crossing over.

On this day, my mother, my sisters and I had decided to have lunch together in my father's favourite Italian restaurant. It is a tiny place with only a few tables and is always packed during lunch time. And that is how it was on this day. Almost every seat was taken and there was only one table left, with a few vacant seats. The waiter guided us to this table, where a man was having his lunch, asking him if we could take the remaining seats. He agreed and so we sat down and ordered a glass of champagne, just like my father would have done. The champagne was served and we were talking, when suddenly the man turned towards us, asking: "Excuse me, if you don't mind my asking: what is it that you are celebrating? Is one of your daughters pregnant?" and my mother replied "No, no, it is not that." So he said: "Well, what is it then that you are celebrating?" "Are you sure, you really want to know?" asked my mother and he said "Yes, I sure would like to know!"

So then my mother turned towards him and said: "The father of my daughter has just died," and while the man was saying "Oh, I am very sorry!" he took my mother's head and very gently pulled her against his chest and held her in his arms close to his heart for a while. When he released her again, very gently, he turned to my older sister and chatted with her about how it is being a lawyer, as it turned out that he was a lawyer himself. Then he turned towards my younger sister and as I was sitting in the middle, our eyes met and I understood in my inner feeling that he was silently conveying the words to me "And you have the latihan. You do not need my consolation," and without speaking a word continued to turn to my sister. He talked to her for a few minutes about Dubai, where she was living at that moment and where he had also worked. Soon after he paid and left the restaurant.

One or two weeks later my mother had the wish to track him down and to talk to him a little bit, as this had been such a special moment for her. She managed to find him and called him up in his law office, reminding him of where they had met and on what occasion. Apparently the phone call was very short, as the man had almost no recollection of this incident.

From *Reminders of Reality*

HAPPY HUNTING GROUND

~ ANONYMOUS

My father passed away in the mid-eighties after a long illness. I was living abroad at this time, so I did occasional latihan and the usual Selamatans (celebrations/social observances). Having two sons of my own, I was aware of the close spiritual connection that exists in a family, and I always wondered how his inner was doing.

However, I completely forgot the one thousand day selamatan and one morning around 4.30 a.m., during this time period, I had a dream which was quite out of the ordinary in that I seemed to remember everything in detail. Although I did not understand it at the time, I was aware of feeling a great happiness throughout. My father was a horse lover and we always had a horse at home from the earliest I could remember, even during the World War II years. My dad knew a lot about horses, and among his friends he was the expert when it came to anything to do with horses.

In my dream, my Dad came riding a white stallion which I recognized and with two other horses on a string. Due to a back injury, my father had quit riding in his late fifties and yet in the dream he was much older. He rode right up to me and said, "Son, I need to get these horses shod." At that moment, my Subud brother Sebastian appeared, the only Subud person I was aware of who knew how to shoe a horse.

Naturally, I asked him whether he could help my Dad, which he was more than willing to do. After Sebastian had taken care of the horses, my Dad thanked him, turned to me before leaving and said, "I am on my way."

For a long time I wondered about this dream and received no real answer. I even visited Sebastian a year later but no light came my way. I even speculated that maybe my father was burdened with the horses because of his attachment to them.

Then, one day out of the blue, the answer came: my father now had all that he needed to return to the Happy Hunting Ground.

From *Reminders of Reality*

MY FATHER'S DEATH

~ ANONYMOUS

I always had a difficult relationship with my father and before his death had become somewhat estranged from him. His chaotic turbulent life in many different countries had a very damaging effect on me and my two brothers. I had left home early although I was fortunate to find the latihan when I was only 18 which healed me and later enabled me to build a more stable family life of my own.

Family life with my parents had been dysfunctional and my father's alcoholism and hasty second marriage following my mentally ill mother's suicide complicated the situation further. It was like living in a Victorian melodrama. He and his second wife lived some distance from me and my husband; traveling was difficult with our small children and I had little contact with him.

However, it was during his final illness that I had an experience that I would never have thought possible considering our relationship. One day there was a knock on my front door and to my surprise on the doorstep was a lady who told me she was the new regional helper who had just arrived in our region. She had found my address in the Subud Directory and had felt compelled to visit me. I invited her in and explained that I and my husband were just off to latihan in the small group in the country we belonged to at that time but she was welcome to join us.

This group consisted of several elderly ladies who all invariably had silent latihans although they were very sincere and respectful of the latihan. I and the visiting regional helper joined in this latihan. Suddenly the ladies burst forth into beautiful singing and a powerful energy swept over us. In this latihan I saw a very large air balloon and was made to embrace it and attempt to push it upwards. It was extremely heavy and I did not think it would ever get airborne as it was so heavy. Nevertheless I was made to continue to struggle with it and at last as the singing reached a crescendo I felt the balloon break free and observed it floating high above us. The ladies said they had not had such a strong latihan for ages! After we finished latihan we all went home and as soon as I got through the door the phone rang. It was my sister-in-law who had just had a phone call from the hospital who had told her my father had died at exactly the time we were having the latihan. As this happened in the days before mobile phones and we had not been informed by the hospital that my father's death was imminent. We had no expectation that he was about to die. I felt that as the only Subud member in my family at that time I had been used to help him leave his body and the regional helper's latihan had added power to our little group. She had no idea my father was so ill. Later on I had a series of other latihan experiences with my father when I was shown the progress his soul had made after he died.

From *Reminders of Reality*

LIGHT IN THE KITCHEN

~ MANUELA MARTINAITIS

Marcus, my father, died of cancer in 2006. It was a quick cancer – he was ill for two months. I went to see him in the hospital – I knew he was dying.

The next week I woke up in the morning and went down to the kitchen to make coffee. Everything was normal… And then there was light in the kitchen, a soft light, and everything was quiet. It was as if time had stopped. It was a few seconds of total stillness… no noise, no movement… it felt as though I was the only thing left alive.

"Papa?"

I felt in my heart that he was visiting me and maybe saying goodbye. I felt that this unusual stillness was from him. I knew time had stopped for a few seconds. I went on with my day, but I was waiting for news and then the hospital called to say that he had died.

The stillness and soft light I had experienced made it easier for me to accept his death.

After he died he communicated with me frequently. I'd get a strong warm feeling in my heart. I had sudden flashes of insight, knowledge and precognition. I joined Subud because he kept nagging at me to do so. And the strange thing is when I got my membership card my name was written in his writing.

WHERE HAVE YOU BEEN?

~ MELINDA WALLIS

My father passed on years ago, at the age of 90. It was sudden. I didn't even get to go to his funeral.

We weren't particularly close, but of course he was my "daddy!" (In those days, it was the mother's job to raise the kids.)

On rainy night a few years ago, I was sitting in the car outside a store. A man came out of the store, walking with a gait and posture SO much like my father's. All of a sudden it was as if my Father was right there!

"Where have you been all these years?!" I cried out (inwardly).

"I've been here with you all along", said my father's voice inside me.

Death doesn't necessarily separate us.

WHEEE!

~ MICHAEL THOMAS

I had arrived in Wollongong, Australia from the USA and been at the bedside of my dying 95 year-old father for three days now. By the fourth day I could no longer delay other urgent family business in Canberra which is a two and a half hour drive from Wollongong. With great reluctance I made the trip to Canberra and arrived back at my father's bedside in the late afternoon of the same day, minutes after he had passed away.

At this time there were four of us sitting quietly with Dad: my stepmother, my sister, my brother and myself. Of the four, only my brother and myself were in Subud and my brother had sworn off the latihan 2 years earlier after nearly 40 years in Subud. Suddenly the latihan was there and it was extremely powerful, so powerful that I knew it could not be stopped. I looked across the room to my brother and could see he was also experiencing the same latihan. We realized that we could not continue the latihan in the room with my sister and stepmother. Luckily however there was a balcony off my father's room and we mumbled our excuses and stepped outside.

Once there I began to experience the most powerful latihan I have ever had. I was literally pinned in a column of white light and felt unable to move at all. Suddenly, in my peripheral vision I saw a little golden globe about the size of a golf ball. It was hovering there looking back into the room where Dad lay. I say looking but it had no physical features and of course, the curtain was closed into the room. I don't know how but I recognized that it was Dad… but a different Dad than the hard materialistic man I had known. This Dad was full of innocence and sweetness and I was reminded of how my mother used to describe Dad when she first met him.

Suddenly Dad spoke, not to me but to himself, "Wow that was interesting, I wonder what's next!" He then turned and saw the column of light that I was in and said. "Oh that's where I have to go!" and jumped into the column of light and I swear he said something like Wheeee! as he shot up the column and disappeared. The latihan abruptly finished.

A couple of things shocked me about this experience. One was the absolute innocence of Dad no longer hampered by his worldly senses. Another was the fact that my father had opposed my membership in Subud for many years. In fact, we had barely spoken for more than 10 years after I was first opened and he had always refused to let my mother be opened (she was opened on her death bed – my brother and I made sure of that).

So how could this experience happen? I expect it has something to do with our latihans (my brother and I) but leave that final understanding to another time. For me it showed that we can move on after death in a much more peaceful and happy way once we are free of our material body. As for my brother, he came back to latihan. What more can I say?

TRAVELING WITH FATHER

~ DEVIN HARRISON

We never travelled much together,
mostly had a propensity for choosing
different directions, as did others
of his generation and mine. I never
thought it mattered, a conciliatory
word, in passing, often sufficed
to bind us through the years. Once
however, shortly before he died,
and penchants aside, we shouldered
up to an oak kitchen table where we
spread our maps, combined forces,
hatched imaginary forays into neutral
lands, planned to visit Japan together.
Immediately, a vigilant Samurai spied us,
unleashed his ancient sword, struck
my father blow. He fell. I held him
as he bled into the dusk of a crimson
floating world. It was touch and go.
Without that martial pose, his spirit
wavered, lanced by a more fecund
worldview. Of course, we never went,
dispositions don't shift that quickly.
But the point is we momentarily broke
common ground, transcended differences,
as we did later when he finally died,
discarding his armor once and for all,
leaving me his kindred, wounded spirit.

SAYING GOODBYE

~ DEVIN HARRISON

When you said goodbye, I was across the world
in an icy, editorial room of newspaper in Seoul,
blowing glass like steam across my glasses. To

reach the cradle of the outmoded phone you called me on,
I sat atop a large, oak desk with a thick
glass protecting it and yelled like Koreans yell,

into the receiver as if my lungs and the distance demanded it.
As I hung there hearing your news, the plate glass
on which I sat cracked suddenly, the sound that ice

makes on the surface of the lake when you step on it,
and I fragmented. Tiny lucid shards entered
my blood, coursed through the arterial walls,

splashed in the cavernous hollow of my being.
I have been on ice before, know how at its weakest points,
it yields, splinters outwards from the point of impact,

its nerve paths suddenly, displayed, transparent and raw,
know how in an instant, everything held firm,
is disassembled, know that when the receiver

was re-cradled, the only sound heard was my body
plunging through the deceptively fragile plain of belonging

REQUIEM FOR MY FATHER

~ IRENA OLENDER

I sing you a Requiem, father,
For peace between me and you.
Your life has passed,
And, free woman at last,
I can choose what to do with you.
Weep for yourself, dear stranger.
I've mourned your loveless life
With sorrow and tears
For long wasted years,
 Ravaged by anguish and strife.

Rest calmly and quietly, father.
Your life has been noisy and sad.
It is clear to me now,
You did not know how
To nurture the good things you had.
Weep for yourself, dear stranger.
I've mourned what could have been,
The feelings we had
The words never said,
The richness of life never seen.

Sleep softly and easily, father.
Soothe the pain in your soul.
Our travel is done,
My life will go on,
I've grown understanding and whole.
The weeping is over, dear stranger.
I've mourned your empty space.
As you blend with the dust,
I know, that I must
Remember, and leave you with grace.

I sang you a Requiem, father.
Its music has set us both free.
Gently have I
Said my final goodbye.
There's peace between you and me.

ORHAN

~ LILIANA WILLIAMS

Why didn't you wait?
In your selfish haze of despair
Did you not think for a moment of me? That I might grow and learn
Then seek and find you?

You underestimated the loyalty of youth
The unbreakable link of kinship —
In your hurry to end your desperate existence

How I fantasized
In adolescent naiveté
Of our warm reunion!
But one cannot reunite without the other.

Many times I wanted to follow you
Into the quiet world of nothingness
To escape, as you had.

You deserted my world with your sad surrender
Your meeting with death left me behind,
Feeling eternally
Stood up.

THE OLD KING
TO MY FATHER & MY DAUGHTER

~ EMMANUEL WILLIAMS

We have come to pay our respects
to the old king
in his little white palace
close to the sea
where roses bloom in yellow praise
walls remember candlelight and saints.

Today the old king
sits thin and frail on his throne.
His voice speaks from a heart so hushed
that words surrender to the silence they arise from.
You study his stiffening knuckles
his tentative step
with a child's dispassionate gaze.
You draw him a picture
of sunlight and rain
and the house where you live
as queen of the summer leaves
and the palace is filled with your rippling talk
the innocent light in your hair.
You reach for the world
the old king is slowly relinquishing
as his life draws into itself
like a symphony rinsed to its primal theme.

If he were here, down on the shoreline
he'd crouch in the breakwater lee
watching you wonder at details
wet stones brown as chestnuts
strands of net and kelp
damp limb of a dismantled dollie.
Then he'd lift his gaze
to contemplate the long horizon
where distant sea-birds ride the wind
and disappear.

The Visitor

Bapak had a letter from Japan telling about a member who had been dead for forty days, or maybe it was three months, and who came and joined in a Latihan again. It happened that during the Latihan one of the members was still outside. He had not yet gone in, feeling as though he wanted to wait for a Subud member who had not yet come. Sure enough one did come. When the man saw the new arrival, he realized that this member had died and had already been dead for forty days or maybe three months, but being so startled he forgot that. The one who had just arrived even spoke to him: 'Oh, you're still outside, not doing the Latihan.' 'Yes, I was waiting for you.' 'Ah, I was expected. Let's go in.' They, then, joined the Latihan.

During their Latihan together this man was incapable of asking any questions. It was as though he was gagged. He went on with his Latihan, and when it was finished he was invited to leave with the visitor: 'Let's go back together, shall we need a taxi?' 'No point in that,' he replied. 'Let's walk.' The man's house was quite near. The visitor said 'I just have a message to give you. I've left my wife behind, and her children are still small. I'm asking you to help. Find some work for her, for my wife. Have pity on my children whom I have left while they are still young. That's my message, and here you are, home. Good night.'

Yes, they had reached his house and the visitor walked away. Only after entering his house did the man remember that the other had already died. Then he thought, 'Oh, in that case I'll go to his wife's place at once.' He went to the wife's house, and then promised to look for work for her, with the result that eventually she got a job.

> Bapak
> Cilandak, Indonesia
> November 24, 1973 (73 CDK 15)

GRANDPARENTS

RITA MAE – A WONDERFUL WOMAN

~ ARVIN LYNES

I was in Indonesia for my father-in-law's funeral. Then I was called and told that my grandmother was dying. I spoke to her for the last time and then was called back again about 15 min later and was told that she had died.

I walked across to the latihan hall to do latihan for her. She'd been such a great grandmother. I was desperate to find out how she was doing and if she had connected with her husband, my grandfather, who had died twenty years earlier and whom she had missed terribly.

So I did my latihan, and then I wasn't sure how to connect with her. The simplest question I could come up with was "Where is my grandmother at this time?" I was astonished and touched – I became my grandmother on her journey. I began experiencing it through her.

I found myself riding what seemed like a lightning bolt. I was holding the hand of my grandfather and found myself screaming with joy, crying and laughing at the same time. So much joy, so thrilling, it caused me to collapse. It seemed too much for the human body to experience.

It wasn't until the next day that I tried to connect with her again – the first experience was too good for me not to want to try again.

Once again I asked, "Where is my grandmother at this time?" I found myself in this great blue room with a crowd of people. All of the people were blue and they glowed like light bulbs. They looked the same, not physically – they all glowed. She was there. She was the same color. She seemed to have her arms wrapped around the whole room. I knew somehow that these were all people she'd known in her life and they were all there to greet her. There was a feeling of love that filled the room, that made it warm in a strange way.

Then that experience ended.

Next day I went to the latihan hall and did it again – I asked, "Where is my grandmother at this time?"

She was riding the lightning bolt again. She was travelling.

I felt there were hands in me, touching my organs. I told myself, "They are washing my organs." It was not uncomfortable. It was a necessary preparation.

Then that experience ended.

At this point I started feeling guilty... Maybe I was peeking in on something I shouldn't have been. This feeling was still there the next day and I asked the same question, "Where is my grandmother?" Again I did latihan.

This time she greeted me.

I asked her if it was okay for me to be doing this.

In her southern accent she said, "God allows what God allows."

She directed me over to where she was having another experience. There were multiple versions of her – greeting me *and* having an experience.

In this experience she was being shown all of creation. I was surprised to find that for her it was like watching a film – from the vastness of the universe to the wonders of the microscopic world. She was crying tears of joy and kept repeating "It's all so great... It's all so great!"

That was the end of that experience.

What was interesting about that was: I wasn't allowed to see the details of what she was shown. I was a little disappointed.

I checked in with her one last time. In this experience she seemed to be very large, very high. Strange to say there wasn't that kind of directionality – but the world seemed to be below her, and she seemed to be getting bigger, rising, expanding. I recognised that part of her was having this experience up in a different location but I was seeing her as near. She said this was God's house and she was going to be allowed to dwell in God's house for a period of time.

This place was colorless – you could see everything everywhere from where she was. There were no walls. It was like outer space. She seemed so large at that point that the world would be like a grain of sand beneath her foot.

At this point I felt satisfied that she was in a great place and I didn't feel the need to continue. The feeling I got was that there are no goodbyes. I know that I could ask at any time and be there again.

SPARK OF LIFE

~ HAMILTON HELMER

In the summer of 1969 my mother, father and I traveled across Canada by train with the end destination of seeing Bapak in Vancouver — so both a wonderful interlude with my parents but also a spiritual journey. I had just graduated from college and had been opened a year and a half earlier.

The stay at the Blue Boy Motor Hotel in Vancouver was our first encounter with Bapak and his family. Ibu was there and this was before Bapak's first heart attack, so he was his more physically robust self. It was a very special time. My mother had the experience in latihan of being surrounded by several of the Indonesian ladies saying "I die, I die". Mom did not think much about it at the time. Shortly after that we took a plane back to Boston and then drove from there to Vermont. On our arrival at my parents' home in Woodstock, Vermont, we were unexpectedly met by Greg Burke, a dear friend of mine and my brother's. He gently informed us that, while we were flying back, my mother's mother had died unexpectedly and that my brother George had gone to her home in Orwell, Vermont to help settle her affairs. We were shocked, as she had been in fine health.

Not long after I had a numinous dream about her. The opening scene was in our family home in Woodstock although in a room unfamiliar to me. The setting was a perfect Last Supper setting with a Caravaggio look replete with chiaroscuro lighting. There was a longish rectangular table on a raised dais. A table cloth was draped across the table. Bapak was the only person seated at the table — in the center of the long side facing out towards my mother and myself, who were standing to the side in the room. As always Bapak's presence was imposing and special. Then, at the door to the room opposite the table, my grandmother appeared. We were quite surprised to see her since we knew she was dead. My mother and I could see that my grandmother was unsettled. She moved in a somewhat disjointed way, and it was clear that something was bothering her. My mother and I then left the room and went to another part of the house to get some champagne (this was my mother's traditional welcome for a special guest). While out of the room we could hear the commotion of Bapak doing a latihan with my grandmother. When we returned with the champagne, my grandmother was transformed. Beautifully attired in a mauve dress she was radiant, warmly smiling and full of the spark of life.

I woke then with a wonderful sense of my grandmother's state that has remained with me ever since. She was an exceptional person who I think loomed large in the spiritual path of our family. She had gone through extraordinarily difficult times in her life and yet emerged positive and worshipful.

GOODBYE GG

~ LEONARD LASALLE

One Saturday night in late June, we were having a party with some friends at our house in French Road. At around midnight, my feelings became filled with the presence of my grandmother. It was so clear and strong that I said to Melinda: "It may sound completely crazy at this time of the night, but I feel I must go and see GG right away."

I left the party, cigarette smoke and loud music to enter the silent darkness of the early summer's moonlit night. Pushed by a feeling of urgency, I rapidly walked towards London Road where the nursing home was situated.

The white-painted Regency building showed no light, except a faint one from behind the curtains of the basement kitchen. A flight of five stone steps led up to the columned porch of the main entrance door. I found it closed and decided not to ring the bell, in view of the time, but to try to climb into my grandmother's room through her sash window. I saw that the top of her window was slightly open and climbed across the short distance from the porch. Then I slowly pushed the window down enough for me to climb over it and land silently in my grandmother's bedroom.

There was enough light, coming from the town's orange streetlights, for me to see around the bedroom. GG's bed was against the right wall, she had her back turned away from the window. I came up close to her and said in a very soft low voice, "GG, it's me, Leonard. I felt you were not well, so I came to see you."

I knelt on the floor close to the head of the bed, kissed her forehead, and found her hand, which I held cosily between my own. "It's good you are here. How did you know? Just stay by me."

I snuggled closer to her. "Yes, like that...." she said. "I don't mind that I'm going to die; in fact I have been waiting for this moment since Edward left me, over 15 years ago now... But I don't want to become a cripple and have to depend on others to look after me," she muttered in a long breath.

"Would you like me to fetch a doctor, GG? Or a priest?" I suggested wrongly, thinking it was what she might have needed.

"No! Neither of them, just you stay next to me," she ordered in a whisper.

I was aware that she was inwardly agitated. Although her body lay motionless, her mind was active and her feelings disturbed. I had been next to people dying on two occasions before and found that the way to be was completely to let go and stay close to the latihan. While still holding her hand, I went into a deep peaceful receptive state and allowed the latihan to flow.

In my field of awareness, I felt the universe surrounding us and heard melodic sounds seem to come from somewhere in its immensity. The musical vibrations reached my vocal chords and we listened together to them soothing and reassuring music that my throat was offering. As the singing went on, my grandmother's breathing became quieter and more regular; we were now together in a space of complete peace where anxiety had no place.

It must have been an hour or more when she suddenly said: "I want to pee, can you help me? I have to turn round; the chamberpot is on the other side under the bed, thank you."

It was painful and difficult for her to move, as her intestines had not been functioning properly for many days and her tummy was enormously blown out, so with much effort I lifted her onto the chamberpot. We managed, and after a while, she made a slight affirmative grunt which I understood as meaning: "I finished!"

I then settled her back carefully into her bed, this time on her right side facing the window. I pulled round the narrow mahogany armchair that stood next to the bedside table and sat in it. She stretched out her tail, frail, shaky hand and rested her cool, dry palm against mine. I reconnected to my peaceful inner state from where flowed harmonious melodic sounds. GG seemed to be listening, her eyes closed, her wrinkled lip showing a slight smile. We stayed like this for quite some time until suddenly she flickered her eyes opened and murmured, "Leonard?"

"Yes GG, I'm here next to you," I responded.

"Could you put some make-up on my cheeks and lips? Tidy my hair? Make me look pretty, and don't forget a sprinkle of my perfume. You'll find everything just there, on the bedside table."

As I did as she asked: on her dry flaky lips I delicately painted the pale pink lipstick, brushed her long hair and tidied it up as best I could, carefully powdered her still–taut, round cheeks and her well–shaped chin.

"Voilà, madame, tu es trés belle à présent."

She liked hearing me talk French to her. Her face showed signs of effort and pain as she wriggled herself back into a comfortable position. With her right hand she took mine again, then looked at me absently. After some time, she gave my hands three gentle squeezes in rapid succession as if to say, "I am going now."

I looked into her watery, shrunken eyes suddenly lit by a fire that seemed to come from inside. All my attention was now directed to the pale pinky blue irises. There I witnessed projecting out the film of her life unravelling rapidly in reverse, all the feeling parts of her existence on earth right up to her birth. I observed, through the intensity of their expressions, a rapid succession of the distinct emotions that she had experienced during her long life: amazement, fear, tenderness, anger, disapproval, joy, love, ecstasy, questioning, stillness, sorrow, hope, approval, pain, acceptance. Then descended, like a delicate sweet scent, a peaceful stillness, which invaded gracefully the room. My hand detected imperceptibly two slight squeezes as if she was saying now, "Au revoir."

I experienced a very very fine musical vibration, starting near my feet and rising through my body… As it reached my chest, throat and head I uttered loudly to my great surprise the equivalent in Arabic of "God is great!"

The ethereal musical vibration rose, taking my awareness with her, leaving my body behind. I went into an immaterial space, wide and peaceful. I understood at that moment that her soul had left her body was now free to rise on its way to another reality.

I open my eyes, which had been closed during these last few minutes, to see my grandmother's body cooling and stiffening in spasmodic jerks. The delicate hand that I been holding was already going cold and I noticed large violet plaques developing under her paper thin skin. Her eyes were now static, staring expressionless.

I rose up slowly crossed her hands on the crest of her chest and drew down her parchment eyelids with the palm of my hand as if I was closing the shutters of her windows, bringing privacy into the space the only belonged to her.

My nostrils detected a heavenly smell in the room, and I felt serene peace in my being. I rearranged GG's appearance, knowing how important it was for her always to leave a good impression of herself. I told a night nurse, who was rather surprised by my presence in the building, that my grandmother had died peacefully, and walked briskly back to our house in the cool morning air.

All the lights were off at home, the party was well over and my family was in the depths of sleep. It did not feel right for me to go straight up to bed, so I walked into our sitting room to do a latihan. It was a good-sized room, faintly lit by the yellowish streetlights that filtered through the bay windows where stood a well-worn, comfortable sofa strewn with soft flowery cushions.

Facing the large window, I stood in the middle of the room, abandoned my heart and mind, thoughts and feelings and placed my awareness in my inner space where neither plus or minus exist, where there is just consciousness in stillness.

After a short time, I felt strongly felt an imposing presence to my left. I turned towards the sofa and to my complete surprise saw my grandfather Edward, who had died fifteen years before, sitting there looking at me angrily. Although I had feared my grandad as a child, I liked him very much and was pleased to see him in our house. But I could see he was disturbed by finding himself in my sitting room! The scene was so ludicrous that I burst into laughter, and the more I laughed, the funnier I found it, as I started to walk round the sofa. Soon grandpa was laughing too. His enormous moustache and heavy thick eyebrows were shaking up and down, moved by the waves of his relaxed laughter.

We were both now in fits, the whole thing was so strange it amusing. I was facing him, still laughing, and noticed that in his sitting position he was slowly rising up out of the sofa in the direction of the sky. My grandfather laughed until he came out of my inner sight and disappeared into his own space. I felt that he had come to find the spiritual connection, which freed him so he could continue on his journey. I felt tremendously lighten and happy and prepared for bed.

As I slipped quietly to snuggle under the weightless duvet, Melinda, coming out of her sleep, mumbled, hardly pronouncing the words: "she hasn't died, has she?"

"Yes, she has, an hour and a half ago."

And before I could share with her what I had just experience, a powerful sobbing shook her whole being. I embraced and held her close to me while she allowed her sorrow to flow out. Inwardly I was not sad, and although Melinda was still heavy in her tears, I felt detached and light.

After some time, I was quite bewildered when I felt an erection developing slowly, vigorously and irrevocably. And I thought to myself, "Come on Leonard! You are a strange fellow, now is not the time for this. Your grandmother has just died and there you are with a flaming erection!"

It didn't know what to do with it as it was bringing down my awareness to its lively need. I went quiet inside and tentatively asked my soul, "Should I follow this impulse?"

The reply was immediate: "Yes, it is important, do follow it."

Close against each other, our cheeks united in the wet of the salty tears that were still flowing, I whispered into Melinda's year, "Darling? You're going to think that I'm completely crazy, but I feel we must come together."

"What… now?" she exclaimed almost indignantly, a pinch of desperation in her voice. Then, she abandoned herself for the natural process to take place, there was no resistance, there was no questioning, we just follow the fulfilment of this unusual journey.

Soon we were taken over by a serene life rhythm that unified us into one feeling. Away from imagination, earthly passions and desires, my awareness grew all around me in a three-dimensional expansion. Consciousness had grown now beyond the house, out and up; I felt the Earth below and directed my attention up towards the Milky Way. As the height of the physical moment came in a burst of powerful energy, I became aware that the spirits of my grandfather and grandmother were being boosted up, through the Milky Way, of which the star-illuminated shape resembled that of a vagina. Melinda was now blissfully sleeping, so I turned around and let myself float away into the currents of my reverie. Reflecting sometime later on this experience, the thought came to my mind: "We come into this world through the gates of the material/physical vagina, we also go back out of this world into the other, through the spiritual vagina."

Now, of course when it comes to sharing the spiritual experiences, I am obliged to use ordinary language and analogies that are only an attempt to give an idea of the spiritual reality I am trying to share.

A few days later the funeral reception was held in our house. The whole family was present and a feeling of lightness and joy pervaded throughout the day. As I been her wish, GG was cremated at Tunbridge Wells crematorium, just a few minutes up the road from number 19; her ashes were later scattered on the Derbyshire moors as Edward's had been before.

A VISION OF MY GRANDMOTHER

~ HALIMAH POLK

When I saw your face
in a dream thirty years after your death
puffed and swollen with weeping
I thought —
that's no face; that's the face of Grief itself!
The woman I had known as a little girl, hidden.
The personality so submerged in this oceanic emotion
that you were no longer you

For a moment your ordinarily white-haired
grandmotherly Slavic face disappears.
I gaze in wonder upon Sorrow herself,
(I had never seen this grief before)
a mask beaten and moulded out of red-raw feeling
shocked mindless by such intensity of feeling
Only a primitive prayer rumbles within.

Are there times in all our lives
when who we are is not visible?
In an unguarded moment, we present
the image of unbearable sorrow or excruciating rage.
No longer our face, but now the face of an icon
imbued with an extraordinary alchemical magic
capable of ravishing the ordinary human heart.

Certainly this imaged icon of my grandmother,
this slivered second of a heightened reality
groans like a bow across the strings of my being
as if I had accidentally stumbled off a high cliff.
Life rushes through my free-falling golden-brown body
and that rushing itself calls out wildly, frantically
 "Oh God, oh God, oh God"
That's no face; that's the face of Grief itself.

Ramadan 1997

BREATH

~ HARRIS SMART

In the war to end all wars, my grandfather was one of those who went out into no-man's-land, bringing in the dead and wounded.

Death came for him one day. Mustard gas drifting across the trenches, burning his eyes and blistering his skin.

It turned his breath to froth, ate away one whole lung and half the other.

But he cheated death. The doctors gave him a year to live, and when he survived that, they gave him another five, then ten. He breathed fifty more and it was the doctors died.

Slowly, carefully was how he went, a frugal man, conserving strength, rationing every breath.

But he accomplished much, as much as any other man more prodigal with breath.

He worked, married, built a house, raise children, saw grandchildren. Doing it all slowly, carefully, measuring every breath.

When he was dying, for no reason that anyone ever understood, my grandfather (not a religious man) said, "My cup runneth over."

Maybe it was because he had done as much with half a cup as most other men do with two.

Illness and Change

When you go through the door of death ~ even though it is death in life ~ you are bound to feel sick, because you are experiencing a change. Every kind of change resembles an illness. So when you feel sick, actually you don't have to complain, because illness is change.

The difference between illness that comes from the latihan and illness that does not come from the latihan, is that illness from the latihan brings change. You need to be sick because you are willed to go through an inner change. This will lead you to death, but in the Subud latihan although you die, you are still alive. Because, as Bapak said earlier, your death is the changing of your content, and this new content already has its vessel. For example, you are dying from a material soul and entering a vegetable soul, or entering an animal soul or a human soul.

You would think that by doing the Subud latihan you should get well. You could say that, but do not forget that the purification and changes within you will require you to feel sick while the process is going on.

Bapak
San Francisco, CA USA
September 9, 1963

SIBLINGS

MY SISTER'S DEATH

~ HARRIS BOEBEL

My sister Beverly (81) died on March 15th, 2011. She, along with the rest of my family, was never involved with Subud and I never mentioned Subud in my infrequent communications. Beverly had been suffering from strokes, seizures, and fractures for the last 15 years, in and out of hospitals and nursing homes. I asked my daughters to do latihan for her. This is their report.... "Sophia, Daniella and I were able to do a simultaneous latihan today at 12:15(P)/2:15(C) for Beverly. We all felt that she was in a wonderful place in heaven. She has shed her pain and doubts. Angels have been and are all around her. Her understanding of God is immense now and she is free at last. There was even joy and laughter... It has been a beautiful day for her and us." signed Hamidah.

Sounds pretty good. Our latihan spreads out among the family, too, without our intention. I felt lighter and the following day during the regular latihan I spent much of it laughing and feeling very good.

SALLY'S PASSING

~ LATIFAH TAORMINA

I want to tell you about the death of my sister, Sally. Sally was eleven years my senior. My half sister really. We shared the same father but not the same mother. And I adored her.

Sally was an incredibly talented artist — but a burdened human being. She could make everyone else laugh, but could not get rid of her own heavy heart. She could really listen when you needed someone to listen, but I don't know if anyone really listened to her. Or even if she could listen to herself. I really don't know all that she went through.

I know that as a young woman, she had debated and debated whether to sleep with a man she'd fallen in love with before they could get married. (People did that back then.) It was during WW II. She was in her twenties and was in London working for the Office of War Information – doing radio communications work. He was an RAF pilot. She decided yes, be with him, and they spent a wonderful night together. The next day, he did not return from his mission. Killed in action. She never quite got over it. She thought it was her fault somehow.

I don't think it was the first awful thing that happened to Sally. But I think it deeply wounded her in a place that was somehow already wounded.

She went from man to man after that. She was always going to get married, but then would break off the relationship. She had abortions, and tried several times to kill herself. I was really not aware of any of this until I was an adult. She was the only other artistic person in the family, and so I felt very close to her. She encouraged the artist in me. And she taught me how to draw. (She herself went to Parsons School of Design and worked as a Fashion Illustrator.) It wasn't till I was out of college that I began to have any clue about what she'd been through or how difficult her life was.

That's when she had yet another very serious suicide attempt. We didn't know at first. The doctors were saying it was some serious liver condition with some very long name. It was later we found out she had swallowed cleaning fluid in the hopes of dying. She was subsequently institutionalized. Her elder brother and his wife went to court to seek legal custody so she could be in an institution near them. I visited her there once. It was a terrible place. I thought it was awful that she was there. But I couldn't spend more time with her. The institution was on the east coast, and I was on the west. She was there for maybe four years. When she got out, she went to live with an aunt in Greenville, South Carolina. There she met an old boyfriend, and at the age of 47, married him.

But on the night of her wedding, she became very ill. She threw up in the john. And he walked out on her. She was subsequently diagnosed with cancer of the colon. Although they caught it in time, it seemed she had no wish to try to get better, and refused any surgery.

I was in Subud by then. That summer, I went to visit her. I felt so strongly to tell her about Subud and even felt to encourage her to get opened. I was not yet a helper and questioned this feeling to almost push her towards Subud. I would test in the john. No, no, go ahead. Push.

So I gave her things to read and then scrounged up some Subud members in South Carolina for a latihan so Sally could be opened. Off we went in a car to find this woman's house out in the country. But as we drove, Sally asked if it would be OK if she just sat outside the latihan. Well of course. Just sit quietly, I said. So I and this other woman who professed to be a helper but seemed to spend most of her time doing Scientology rather than Subud, did latihan in one room, and Sally waited in the woman's kitchen.

I was so aware of my longing for Sally to have the blessing of the latihan that I had great difficulty letting go of this awareness in my latihan. I begged forgiveness of the Almighty that I couldn't be in a more surrendered way. I will just have to accept that this is how it is, I decided reluctantly. I'm just not good at this surrendering.

On the way home, Sally confided that she had felt her tumor move during the latihan! I was astounded! I felt so hopeful, but I could not stay in South Carolina, and the woman helper I had found did not follow up as she had promised.

So Sally experienced the latihan just that once while sitting in the next room.

Months and months later, in November, it was Ramadan. I was living in Bolinas, California – a tiny village on the coast in Marin County. My husband, Alan, had left me, and I wasn't sure where my own life was headed. It was around two in the morning, and I was boiling water for coffee. Suddenly, I had a spontaneous daydream – latihan experience.

This was my "daydream":

I was at Siti Rohana's house in Mill Valley when there was a knock at the door. Rather than sit while Rohana opened the door — I mean, it was her house — I went to the door and opened it.

Sally was standing outside. She was wearing traveling clothes, the way people used to dress up to take a trip. She was wearing a hat, a suit, and carrying a purse. She looked very happy. I was ecstatic.

"Sally!" I exclaimed. "What are you doing here?"

"I just passed on!" she burbled happily. (We were both burbling like two college chums meeting after some years and squealing in delighted high voices with each other)

"Great!" I exclaimed. "How perfect that you should come here because Rohana's a helper and she can open you." And then I turned to Rohana to introduce Sally.

"Rohana! Look who's here. It's my sister, Sally, and she's come here to be opened!" And then I suddenly wondered if you could open someone who'd passed on.

Right then the day-dream stopped, and I found myself saying out loud, "Just say Allah, Sally. Just say, Allah."

I was quite shaken. Had my sister just passed on? Oh, it couldn't be that I experienced my sister's passing, I thought. I'm not a helper. I'm not anybody. It must be a sign that I should call Sally in the morning to tell her not to be afraid to pray to God. I knew she had no wish to be a hypocrite, to be someone who wonders about whether God exists, and then, at the last minute, prays just in case. But I also knew that was just her own head-trip. So I planned to tell her to not feel shy to pray. I'd tell her it's really OK to say something like: "Dear whoever you are, if you're there, help me now." Like that. That would be just as good I felt.

I noted the time.

The next morning, when I called, Sally had indeed passed on at exactly the time I had that day-dream latihan

A week or so after that, at the end of Ramadan, I was doing latihan with the group in Marin. Rosina Filippelli, one of my Subud sisters who was always there was not there. She was pregnant with her first child, and the last 100 days of her pregnancy had begun. So she was not at latihan.

In my latihan, I suddenly saw my sister Sally walking with Ibu Siti Sumari, Bapak's former wife. Sally was holding a parasol for Ibu – like the ladies did with

Ibu in Cilandak when Ibu would go to latihan hall from the Big House. And they were just strolling and chatting. And Sally was so alive and so happy! And I was in Marin and somehow seeing all this with my eyes shut. And the tears rolled down my cheeks. And I kept saying something that I didn't understand until later.

I kept saying over and over as three separate 'words' :

Mee

Rah

Cull

Mee

Rah

Cull

And then, while I was still seeing Ibu walk with Sally, I saw Ibu suddenly be in front of Rosina. Ibu reached out to pat Rosina's belly. "And how is Rosalind?" Ibu asked.

That was it. I have to tell you that at that time, Rosina was absolutely convinced that her baby was going to be a boy named Maxwell. I had no idea what the child was to be called if it were a girl.

After latihan, I asked Rohana if she knew what Rosina's baby was to be called if it were a girl.

"Rosalind."

And indeed, three months later, Rosalind was born.

Miracle! Miracle! That's what I had been saying. And just in case I might doubt what I was seeing about the next world — that Sally was there and in a wonderful place and with Ibu — I was given proof in this world. I was shown the child that was to come and the name of the child.

So… it is a miraculous place we go to. Even with less than one latihan.

THE COLOURS

~ MANUELA MARTINAITIS

Ever since my brother Albert was a child his life had been hard. In October 1990 he died at the age of 30. He was an alcoholic.

Before he died we – parents, girlfriend and I –were gathered around his bed in the hospital. The doctors told us they were taking him off the life-support systems.

We were crushed, crying and inconsolable. This was my first experience of death. Then I looked at my brother's eyes, and I saw that his irises were like kaleidoscopic areas of beautiful glowing colours, which were moving. For a while as I looked at this vision, I was no longer feeling sad. I was thinking that perhaps he was seeing some beautiful place, the place that he was going to.

It lasted about two minutes and then he died, and the sadness came back and stayed with me for a long time.

Before he died, my brother told me, "It's okay. I'm okay with it." I think these exquisite colors were his way of seeing or showing what was coming. He'd suffered a lot, so maybe he was glad to go.

FOR SUE

~ MALAMA MACNEIL

I burned your papers today.
As I lit the string I'd used to tie them all together
when I moved them (finishing the task you set me)
a year ago and more,
a radio played the Adagio for Strings —
that aching ascension so bound for me to another love, lost.
Fitting, I thought;
one parting reflects all partings.
One irrevocable bond (forged by birth, intention, or sometimes, both),
even broken,
is tied to every other.

Neighbors, lovers, family, and friends, we sat with you;
promised we would see you to the end, and kept our promise.
Your friend dreamed a great horse came for you, and free of illness,
you rose and mounted,
riding into the mist at the mountain-tops of some Chinese landscape.
We brought flowers, hung the room with celebration and repose,
and tried to ease you on your way.
Born to the sign of the Horse, you died as you lived, by choice,
with grace and wit, and at the end,
I said I loved you, and would miss you
(how little then I knew how I would find you missing);
and believing the dream, I said I would be glad to see you go.

I've hung the prayer flags from your dying room
(in memory now, so full of quiet life) across the entrance to
my new room, the one in which I can find no place for your ashes,
the one that is full of reminders of you.
The strings between the flags broke as I hung them, and had to be re-

tied;
the knots have made them stronger then before.
Now they flutter their five colors, offering to the horses of the wind
(even in the shelter of the yard) their blessing:
May the rain fall at the proper time.
May the crops and livestock be bountiful.
May there be freedom from illness, famine and war.
May all beings be well and happy.

Mourning you, I dream now our lives that simple,
and gracious death seems just the tug that snaps the cord.
May we, all, be well and happy.
May we be well, and happy.
May we be well, and happy.

THE BREAK ~ FOR ELLA

~ RIANTEE RAND

On the first day of the New Year
I jumped into the winter ocean
casting off wishes for all my friends.
And you, Ella,
leaned into me more than before.

The earth tilted as I splashed
and splashed
many times
out
of
my
mind,
entering the beginning place
for all of us,
forgetting it was also the ending one.

The wind had stopped that night
and we watched the crescent moon
play hide and seek behind clouds
then, reclining on its back,
it curled up into the ocean,
and moved the remaining light
into translucent shapes,
shades of knowing
who Ella was.

Trailing the moon,
Jupiter kept a bright eye on us all.
At midnight,
the young ones dove in
two, three and six times
then, like devils out of the box
hopped around on the sand.
Later they gathered around the bonfire
shaping memories from the smoke.

Startled when the dark of night
exploded into all colors,
we howled our pleasure
at the new year that promised
the earth's deepest turning,
an opening of sky
and a wash of ocean green.

I learned when I went home
that you had left just before the moment we jumped in,
drifting into the forgetting place
as the icy cold water
slapped our bodies into recognition.
You let go of the old year
knowing that on earth
you had no more business
with the new.

Three days later on the bluff
we gathered at the place
where your coffin awaited
to be lowered into the grave.
The icy cold wind drilled into us
stealing our words,
only your rabbi was bold enough

to challenge the wheezing of that gale
and offer us a length of your life, Ella,
your love of it that accepted
the good as well as the bad.

She raised images
that brought you back
for an instant
in all your radiancy;
I was along on that Mikvah you called
to de-cord yourself from the love obsession,
that addiction of yours so deeply rooted into the fathers.
I was there
as we all put our hands on you, lying on the sand.

Over the years I heard all your stories
and I repeated them to you after you lost Ella
and you were so delighted to learn
what a wonderful being she had been.

Our bodies moved closer to each other,
like penguins we tightened our circle,
a few lost their grief into the weather,
and I saw you from the corner of my eyes
standing there by your son
when his voice broke into song,
your smile full of tender mystery
as you weaved the release
of him and all others.

Yes Ella, we are now the mothers
of the mothers,
the mothers of the fathers,
it's our turn to face the wind
and spin our sorrow into song.
You glide again like an eagle,

a little farther this time
into the great plains of your ancestry.

Yes, it was us that were lowered
into the ground,
us we shed tears for,
those tears washed away the sins of the fathers,
and all the sins of silence.

You invited us Ella,
one more time and maybe the last,
into this perfect light,
with this perfect love in our hearts,
at this perfect moment of time,
in this place where we could do nothing
but the absolute right thing.

Your blessings
on a winter day.

Three Becoming One

It is clear that it is your thinking that makes the distance between the line of life and the line of death. Whereas, in actual fact there is none.

You were already there before you came into existence, and you will still be there after you are gone from here and have disappeared again, it is the same thing.

That is called trimurti; three becoming one. It is a unity consisting of three phases.

Bapak
Cilandak, Indonesia
April 14, 1974

SPOUSES/ PARTNERS

DEATH . . . OR BIRTH?

~ ANONYMOUS

My husband had been ill with cancer for quite some time. He wanted to be at home for the last part of his journey in life, so for the last few months I was helped by nurses by day and by night. These very kind and compassionate ladies would show me what I needed to know and because of their kindness (especially the night nurses) they cheered me up. One day a nurse, someone I hadn't seen before, came in and explained to me that everyone else was away on holiday. She then went about her business of checking my husband while I was in the kitchen preparing food for my children. Before long she came to me and said, "It's time". I went to the bedroom and sat beside the bed and the nurse (I think her name was Helen) stood in the doorway and began to speak to my husband as though he was giving birth. I looked at her and thought *No, no. You have it wrong. He is dying.* "Go slow," she said. "Don't panic." I think she even began to count him back from eleven — ten, nine, etc. *How can this be? This is not a birth.* Then my husband passed away, and she said, "That was a very good death," and after some time she was gone. All of a sudden, there was a huge commotion on the roof and I ran outside and saw that the roof was covered in birds. I could not see a single tile on the roof for birds, some of which I had never seen before. I ran back inside and, after sitting beside my husband, thought This is the **reality** of Life, One day I too will die. After 27 years I am still trying to come to terms with that. Since my husband's passing, I have been witness to two more deaths and with each it seems that maybe one's passing can be seen as a Birth after all.

From *Reminders of Reality*

PEACE

~ ABRAHAM CALMAN SPIVAK

Sandra was dying. My wife had been diagnosed with cancer. She was such a fine person, a true mate and partner to me, very inclusive and good with people, a loving mother and wife who conveyed to me and our children that fun can accompany almost any activity – and we did have that, especially imparting to us the profound message that even small things can have consequences. Sandra took this news of her terminal illness well, and continued to take care of what she needed to do, and while I did, too, I became numb.

Our oldest child was married now to a fine young man, our younger child was about to complete high school and our youngest was in middle school. Sandra was very concerned how her death would affect them, and we often talked about this at length. I promised that I would do everything I could to see that they were okay, and this meant so much to her. I could feel the release of fear and tension as her body relaxed when I made sure she knew she could rely on me as she had always done to do everything that was needed.

We were given twenty-one months with her. And we lived normally, Sandra remaining active and the family doing things together as we had always done. Sandra and I went to the Subud Menucha Retreat to enjoy the peace and serenity of that place and to the California Regional Congress, on both occasions for her to be able to say goodbye to her many friends. We regularly did latihan with our Subud group, and she and I also shared latihan together. We made a point that she would be taken care of at home as the time approached. When she became too weak to go to the group, the women came and did latihan with her at our house. It was a blessing for her.

We went to family therapy to ease that coming time for the children. It was an honor to hear what the children had to say and how clear and accepting they were. They said that was due to the way their mother had responded and was facing this calamity. I was so proud of them. But for me personally, although I seemed outwardly to be managing well, it was almost by rote and habit. Though I appeared as normal as ever, I was totally without any feeling, only numbness.

On that last day we were all gathered around her bed. Even in these last hours

Sandra had remained connected to us, grunting to let us know, because she could no longer speak. And as she drew her last breaths, we were saying goodbye, and thanking her and telling her that we loved her. Then it was over. And in a kind of slow motion people began leaving the room.

I stayed, rooted. I thought I was prepared for this moment. But there is no preparation. My insides had broken to pieces. No one knew, and I was desperate that no one know, but I was shattered by inner turmoil. My bewildered head was in a whirl, my body felt paralyzed with anguish. I had no idea how I could stand this. I was feeling such total loss it was impossible for me to see how I would be able to handle anything. How could I take care of what was needed, and all that I had promised Sandra? I was ready to collapse and throw my hands up in despair.

As I edged out into the hall trying to avoid being seen, I realized everyone was in the other part of the house. And the idea immediately occurred to me that if I closed the door at the entry to the hall I would be isolated. I could try to do latihan even though it seemed impossible to me in my condition. I could try to ask for help to be able to take care of things, to be able to be "strong" for my wife and children, to be as I had promised. So I stood there now and asked for the latihan to come. The instant I asked, in that very instant peace enveloped me. Immediately all the turmoil and anguish and doubt vanished. Immediately! It's like I was alive again, and knew I could handle whatever was needed, and I would, and that all would be well. I was amazed, here given evidence again of the power of the spirit. I was so grateful and am again and again for this gift of the latihan. I opened the hallway door and joined my family and knew we would be okay as Sandra wanted, with my arms around them.

ON THE DEATH OF MY HUSBAND
~ LATIFAH TAORMINA

I am here and not here.
He is gone and not gone.
I call his name

I laundered everything that touched him.
I threw out all the stained pillows.
I bagged all the torn clothes —
Torn to help them go on and off easily.

I will tell you later about washing and wrapping his body
In the early dawn hours as the warmth left it.

I will tell you later about the rose petals I put between the white sheets we wrapped round him.

I will tell of you later about the clump of earth I placed at his navel to give his body burial in cremation — and the prayer that came as I did that —
And the vibration that filled the room.

I will tell you later about sitting beside the bed when it was done
And reading Ya Sin from the Qur'an he gave me so long ago.

But now I barely know how to tell you.

I have only words.

They are not enough.

January 2014

TRANSFORMING FEAR, LOSS OF A SOUL MATE

~ LUSIJAH ROTT

I was Husain Chung's partner the last five years of his life. It was dense in its intensity, a period of enormous growth, with profound healing and change on a deep structural level. Loving and being loved — it seemed akin to how the sunflower opens fully and follows the sun. I was childlike again, giddy, with lots of laughter, fun, feeling extraordinary emotional safety. In our time together, I had an experience related to the Zen koan: experience your original face before you were born. I knew that I could be *that* with Husain. It was like the fairy tale that I had long thought was just a childish dream.

There was a cloud lurking however—our age difference.

Around a year and a half before Husain died, we had a conversation about the high probability that he would die before me, being 22 years older. I was still at the Institute of Transpersonal Psychology, close to finishing a masters in counseling psychology. As part of the creative expression specialization, I was required to do a project with personal meaning, using creative expression. I chose to work with my anxiety related to our age difference. I had spent hours recording vocals, cello, poetry that I had written, and doing the sound mixing. It was a love song. The problem was that the work had not addressed the gut wrenching anxiety I had — *this could end any day*. Husain agreed to talk to me about this fear. It was a conversation about a serious matter. I needed something from him, I didn't know what, and he didn't know how to help me. All I knew was that I had a sense of panic and sadness when I thought about our age difference and that he would in all likelihood die before me. I recorded the conversation and have had the perspective of time to revisit this conversation, and be struck at how true it turned out. I asked Husain what he would say to me, seeing me grieving after his death.

Husain: (very long pause) I just . . . (silence) that's my answer, not saying anything. It's not any words. That's good . . . the experience brings you close to God. It's part of the experience of creation. Experiencing the mortality. That is the meaning of life, part of the deeper meaning of God's creation to experience all that. Whereas the angels don't. They don't experience sadness, they don't experience all that. They're so angelic, they never . . . . they're jealous of the humans. And you... that is the ultimate of the human experience between heaven and earth. When you experience the human experience, you experience heaven and earth. You experience what is God, love, and its destruction and its absence. (Pause) And so you feel the immortality of the soul. (Pause) You experience your own immortality and mortality at the same time, it's quite an experience. It's not something like the beginning and ending of a symphony, you see the whole thing. You know from the first movement to the last and the whole totality of it, the 3D of it. You didn't just experience this aspect of life, you experienced the total thing, everything about it and it's in you.

This was not helpful to me at the time, although hearing this well after Husain's death has had resonance. In this conversation I kept pushing him. "What are you going to say to me, grieving when you die?" Finally, I actually finally got down prostrate on the floor. After a very long period of silence Husain said:

Well, truthfully, I can't say I'm not happy of dying. I'm very pleased. Finally that moment came. (Pause) I think it will be a grand experience for you though, more for your life than anything else — when I die. Yeah, I died in peace. If it wasn't for you, it would be a different kind of death. I never had happiness like this. Never tasted it. I never really tasted life like this... that love was a kind of happiness that I've never experienced. I couldn't have said, you know that I've never been loved before or loved before. I did. But it's not like the soul mate love I have.

As I was on the floor, I felt what I would have said to him, were the tables turned — a sort of expansive happiness. Out of this, I understood that for Husain it would be good. It took me out myself to feel how it would be for him. This talk that we had, a year and a half prior to Husain's passing, stayed with me. It transformed the fear and panic to knowing the rightness of Husain leaving this plane when the time came as part of his soul's journey. It was grief work done before the fact.

When Husain was diagnosed with stage IV lung cancer, we continued very important conversations of love, support, and gratitude that our life paths had crossed. I knew that he would not recover from this, I told him I would walk this journey with him, continue to love and support him, and do what I could to make sure he would be comfortable. Among other things, Husain also told me he would continue to hug me, asking was I sure I would know? Husain died a month after his diagnosis. I really felt that he made the decision to leave his life just as pain was becoming intolerable. He was conscious until the end, sitting on the bed, he just asked to lean back. As he leaned back, I felt moved to play particularly beautiful Islamic calls to prayer that one of my colleagues had given us during the previous Ramadan; Husain lost consciousness and never regained consciousness.

In the first hour after Husain's death, as I was sitting with his body, playing these same beautiful Islamic calls to prayer, I very suddenly had an overwhelming sense that Husain's spirit had filled the room, like he was dancing, and I could sense that he had his arms around me. I cried and then laughed in joy. Since then, I have several times felt Husain's arms around me at times that I have struggled with missing him. Through tears, suddenly, I feel him close and I sense his arms around me. I have felt a wave of joy and gratitude — he kept his promise.

The night after Husain died, there was a latihan and at some point I felt Husain invite me to where he was. It was so wide, powerful — words are completely inadequate — that I could not fully embody the intense energy of this experience and I stepped away inwardly. I have regretted that I stepped away. This experience meant that in the first couple weeks after Husain's death, there was a part of me that was filled with wonder and joy for him. The many challenges and hurdles he had had in his life were over. A part of me was able to celebrate for him — soul return to where he truly belonged.

This didn't mean that I didn't experience the psychic whipsaw, jolt of separation. It showed up in different ways, like all the circuits were utterly blasted, vacancy, stunned, drifting, confused — all very typical early grief responses. I felt that I lost short-term memory for a while. However, in the year and a half since Husain died, I have never felt "absence". There have been times that the contact feels very close, I have felt the thinness of the veil, even the experience of an energetic interwining, a continued soul dance, briefly and then crushing sadness — I am still here. There have been times that I have asked a question that I really wanted his opinion about and then heard his voice internally. Not the physical voice as much as his familiar message. There have been times that I have wished to share a triumph and the joyous result. As soon as I think of wanting to tell Husain, I also feel, he already knows. He is smiling across the veil.

In the conversation we had a year before Husain's death, he mused about loss of a soul mate.

Well what happens when one of the soul mates dies. That is more an incredible experience when two people are not soul mates and one dies. Vastly different. We touch on the transpersonal constantly in so many experiences. We live both lives, the outer and the inner… the immortal and the mortal.

Many (most?) could not understand looking from the outside why Husain and I were together. We were so very different, different age, life history, ethnicity, physical stature and capability, different personality and temperament. I had spent my life working in biomedical research, he had been one who followed his own muse, and crazy it had been at times. It might be difficult to find two people who would have less cause to have any cause for interaction, not to mention a relationship! And yet I felt like I was deeply and joyously home when I simply came into close proximity to Husain. I felt this closeness as sensing some essence that was as tangible to me as tasting chocolate. Clear, recognizable and the sensing has continued after Husain's death, a way that I have known... he is close.

I remember hearing a story about Bapak's comments on soul mates, that in this lifetime it may not be even possible for soul mates to meet, as the age, ethnicity, geographic location may be so far apart. I had heard that he had made this comment at a time that he was testing with an Indonesian woman who was having marital problems. Bapak confirmed that her husband was "younger", not a fit, but that if she treated him with love and care, perhaps she might come closer to finding her soul mate – later. I felt I had been given this gift. Both of us felt profound gratitude that we had had this brief spell together. What would be our soul's journeys in the future?

Husain believed the two of us would be given work together in the future.

What's it like on the other side? Husain talked before his death that he had a big job waiting for him. He expressed even excitement! A while after his passing, I put the question out to him, "So, what are you doing now? What is the job?"

After a pause of feeling quiet, waiting for some understanding, I felt an answer — that it is not possible for me to understand the answer. "What are you doing?" doesn't fit. There is a whole different paradigm.

On Psychodrama. Not too long after Husain's death, working as an intern therapist, I used psychodrama, a personal growth modality that Husain had been a master of. I realized that although I had learned a great deal from him, I needed more training to be able to use this modality. He had been intuitive and spontaneous in his work. It was like a locked box to me, frightening, requiring a courage I didn't think I possessed. I signed up for a training workshop with the Hudson Valley Psychodrama Institute. The actual original stage used by its inventor had been moved to the site. I walked around the stage that had been built by Moreno, the same stage Husain had experienced psychodrama. The practice was so different than Husain's, who had practiced in the era of the late 60s during the flowering of the human potential movement and personal encounter. He had been willing to allow the unfolding of dramas spontaneously. The evolution of psychodrama has become more structured with less room for quick intuitive movement; there are now strong safety structures. It is safer and yet lacks the spontaneity of his work. When I came back I was confused, thinking, what way is my way, what way is better? I found myself on the hamster's wheel, considering, thinking, coming to no conclusion. As I was climbing into bed a week or so after my return, I threw it out. "What about this Husain?" I felt surprised, thinking, *what am I doing?* Amazingly, I could hear Husain's voice and amusement at me trying "figure it out". He said *the most important thing is to be fully present with whoever you are with. Feel your own inner connection, alive in your inner feeling. The rest of it is just techniques."* This was his mastery, the way he himself lived and worked with people and the fundamental teaching he gave me—to be connected, trusting, courageous. This memory, the feeling of what this means continues to evolve, will always remain with me.

Forgiveness. **H**usain had relationships in which others whom he loved and cared about had hurt him. As Husain's partner, I hurt for and with him when some of these came up while he was alive. It seems that death can heighten these feelings for the living.

I asked Husain about this. "Do you feel angry at some of the people that hurt you?" And then I just let the question go, I didn't think about anything, I didn't try to figure out what he might say. There was just emptiness, open receptivity, no expectation. A few moments later, the answer came not in words but again in feeling. I can only describe the feeling. The space of soul is totally different, there are no heart feelings "I've been hurt." There is a vast understanding of the beingness of those who hurt him, a greater compassionate about where they're at, a compassion for the human condition of living in earth realm. Just after this, I experienced a feeling like soothing water that flowed into my feelings.

On Grief. My experience with Husain's passing has greatly informed my work with clients who have experienced the death of a parent or a spouse. I have witnessed clients move from being incapacitated by grief, barely able to speak, towards integration of the bittersweet of loss. The sweetness is of continued existence of the personal gifts they received from their spouse and how the survivor's life was and continues to be enriched by the one they lost. I have encouraged clients to consider that the loved one exists within them on a cellular level that can be felt in quiet moments — how they laughed, their sense of humor or caring, wisdom, calling into presence the feeling of being loved, touched, kissed. These remain as does the sadness of loss. It is and will always be bittersweet. I have also witnessed that people without spiritual practice have a harder time. I believe one of the great gifts of the latihan is awakening of soul awareness that goes beyond intellect or personality. I have no doubt that this is the reason I have not felt "absence".

Anger and guilt are often a difficult part of the grieving process. I have seen sons, daughters, husbands or wives painfully remembering what they said and didn't say or remembering what they had done and not done. The experience after asking about Husain about whether he was angry at those who had hurt him has been important as I have helped clients work through unresolved issues by bringing in the loving and compassionate presence of the one they lost through psychodrama or simple letter writing.

I have seen in grief group participants that there is guilt associated with the prospect that a husband or wife might seek or find another partner. The surviving partner feels perhaps they are disloyal to consider this. In every instance when therapeutic work has invited the compassionate and loving presence of the spouse who has died into the sessions, the surviving spouse has experienced that their partner wants them to be happy. I have never heard from anyone that the "message" from the deceased spouse is anger or jealous. I experienced this myself when I felt Husain's former wife (who had died) visit me in latihan shortly after Husain and I got together. I had not met her, but recognized her somehow in latihan. It was just the one time and I felt gratitude from her that Husain would be cared for and loved. Since Husain's passing, I have felt an inner knowing that the paradigm of love and soul mate connection after earth life is different than how this is experienced in this life. The connection remains but is of such a different quality that disloyalty, jealousy, "better than" have no place.

There is a wonderful story in the agency where I have worked during my internship, the Center for Living with Dying. This was from a client who had experienced many losses and was asked how she had survived. She replied that each person that she has loved and who has passed on has a room in her heart hotel. That room keeps all the love and memories and will never disappear. The client then added that she can build new rooms for people she will love in the future. I have no idea about what is in store for me; I like the heart hotel idea.

REMEMBERING RAMDHAN

~ MARDIJAH SIMPSON

At dawn on Sunday, June 12th 1994 Ramdhan, my dear husband, died at home in Sydney.

There was a national kejiwaan gathering that long weekend. Ramdhan spent the Saturday at the Subud Hall, coming back home late and happy; happier than I had seen him for a long while as his heart had been troubling him more and more over the years. As I was working all week and needed catch up at home on the Saturday, I had planned to join the gathering on the Sunday and Monday.

He positively glowed as he settled down to regale us, Mursalin, our son and three of our daughters, with all that had happened at the Hall. I offered to cook him his favorite breakfast, for some reason, as I knew he would have been too engaged in conversation to eat. He happily had a late supper of scrambled eggs and we went to bed. We snuggled in under our big doona as the Sydney winters can get cold. I dozed off and he woke me with a message from a visitor at the Hall. I dozed and was woken again as he remembered someone else's message. Finally we slept.

Sometime much later, in the dark of night, he woke me asking for aspirin – the only remedy he ever used to ease his heart. I was well prepared for this ritual and scrambled off to the bathroom, feeling for the mug, the water and the white heartsease in the dark. It fizzed and he gulped it down. It was freezing cold. He felt cold.

"Go and get Mursalin," he said. I knew it was serious and he needed a man to latihan with. I went and woke Mursalin who went to him straight away. I stopped in the kitchen to make hot tea and fill a hot water bottle. The night sky was beginning to fade with the hint of a new day. Up in our room Mursalin was sitting beside his father and we arranged the bottle and gave him the tea. The room seemed very quiet and clear. Ramdhan asked for more aspirin, although he had taken some less than forty minutes before and knew there should be an interval of four hours. I just went and got them for him, I felt quite calm, although I knew that if the first two had not eased his pain, things were serious.

I perched on the side of the bed beside him, holding his left hand while

Mursalin held his right. Ramdhan lay back and I felt quiet inside despite the cold, waiting for the pills to work. Ramdhan talked, he was a great talker. I was so sleepy and cold I just let the words flow around me. I could not be sure if his voice seemed blurred due to sleepiness, happiness, sadness or pain or if he was in some strange state of receiving. The daylight grew in the room. I felt the deepest quietness and my mind switched off yet I seemed to sense or maybe see – with my mind's eye – images, like a William Blake drawing of angelic figures ascending and descending. Then I felt and heard, as if from within my own chest this deep creaking and seemed to see an small, old, solid wooden door with rusty hinges, struggling to open. I felt it was Ramdhan's heart and felt a quiet joy that at last he had broken free of old sorrows. I said nothing. He talked on. We were all cold. I offered to get fresh hot tea and top up the cooling water bottle, and went down to the kitchen. It took me less than five minutes to boil the kettle, make tea and refill the bottle. As I walked back from the kitchen a phrase flashed through my mind – "All we have in common is the latihan and our children" – I felt sad at what I thought to be a negative idea from my subconscious.

Upstairs, Mursalin was standing outside our bedroom. He looked dazed. "I think he's gone" he said.

I went in and could see that indeed Ramdhan had died. I went to him but he was as empty as an envelope left behind when the love letter has blown away.

The rest of the morning was like some stately dance. I felt even calmer – an unearthly calm. My mind quietly clicked into gear and I knew each thing that had to be done.

For my family – I went and woke each daughter gently and told them the news. Then I rang Dahlan, Ramdhan's older son. He said he would come immediately with Harry Armytage, the national helper who was staying with him For the world – I rang the ambulance and described what I had witnessed. They came quite soon, realized they could not revive him and rang the police after hearing that he had not seen a doctor in the past three months.

The girls got up, wrapped in blankets against the freezing blue morning; they floated around the house, just like Blake figures. A young policeman turned up who was quite overwhelmed with the occasion and had to keep ringing someone senior to check on procedure.

A great deal of tea – one of Ramdhan's favorite drinks – was made and drunk. (Later that day, the kettle too died).

Dahlan, Mursalin and Harry had a latihan in the room with Ramdhan's body.

Later Harry told me it had been as if an arrow had flown free and fast up and away into the firmament, leaving no trace behind.

Later still one daughter told me that in the cold dawn she had heard Ramdhan call her name, as if to wake her for school, but she had been so sleepy she kept her head buried under her doona and did not reply. Then another daughter told me that she too had heard Ramdhan come into her bedroom and tell her he was sorry, but he could not make her a wake-up cup of tea this morning. Then I realized that what I had heard – 'all we have in common is the latihan and our children' – was most probably not my thought – but Ramdhan, truthfully telling me how things were now he had left the physical world.

A locum doctor visited but would not sign the death certificate and told me to contact our doctor. I managed to get him on the phone. Later he rang back to say that he had gone into his surgery to check the files but found no sign that Ramdhan had ever let him know of his heart pains. So – he was sorry but he could not sign the death certificate either. This meant I had to surrender his body for a post mortem.

Later we went to the hall for latihan. The news had already spread. Subud members from around Australia who had come for the gathering were there and I found myself having to hold and comfort many of them as their sorrow at his death poured out.

That evening, instead of the planned selamatan there was a special one for Ramdhan. Close friends had arranged flowers and prayers and then anyone that felt to shared their memories of Ramdhan – quite a few were amusing and we laughed. I felt in a dream.

During the week as we waited for coroner to confirm Ramdhan had indeed died of a heart attack we planned the funeral. Days went by. Flowers arrived in sheaves. The local florist's driver had to climb the cliff up our 28 steps to the house each time. By the end of the week the house was ablaze as every vase, jug, basin, bowl and bucket was filled with rainbows of flowers.

A kind Subud sister had rung me on the day of his death to tell me that we need not worry about cooking and for the next week, a different evening meal would arrive at our house prepared by different Subud friend each day.

The children and I talked about the funeral. We knew he had wanted to be buried and managed to find a plot for him at the cemetery on Botany Bay in sight of his beloved blue sea. At first we fooled around with the idea of sending him on his way in just his swimming togs with a spray of seaweed – but decided this might cause a kerfuffle at the gate of heaven. So in the end we chose his best blue batik shirt, slacks and his comfy fisherman's sandals. One daughter donated her blue Amnesty ankle socks (as he had often borrowed them without asking anyway!). Another daughter gave a little white bible, to go at his side. His patche went at the other side. Another daughter gave a little jar of her special honey. I put some jacaranda seeds in his shirt pocket from the tree he had so carefully nurtured in our garden. The undertaker, a blokey guy in a sweater with a (then novel) mobile phone, was plain talking and practical – just the sort of chap Ramdhan would have got on with, accepted all our objects and arranged them with Ramdhan in his simple wooden coffin.

We had the funeral at the graveside, in the sandy dunes beside the Bay. A great many people came; Subud friends from across Australia and some from overseas. A reading from Bapak and from the Koran accompanied the regular words of the Christian funeral. Then there was a big selamatan at the Hall. Somebody said 'Ramdhan would really have enjoyed this'. While the evening sky swirled in a crimson sunset above us all.

Some years later, when I was writing poetry reflecting on Ramdhan, I realized that the date of his delayed funeral – June 17th was the exact date, 37 years earlier that I had first met this man, with whom I would discover the latihan and have five children.

Alice Springs, Australia
March 31st 2011

FAREWELL TO A MARINER

~ MARDIJAH SIMPSON

Last night the sun set and the moon rose
Sailing the soft ocean of the western skies
Fragile as a Viking ship carved from a walrus tusk
Carrying your warrior's soul to safe harbour.

Last year I planted jacarandas: seedchildren of your tree
in memory to mark each corner of your green land
then rode the descendant of a Dyak death ship
up the green arterial waterworld to your lagoon.

Two years ago I launched your husk, snug in its craft
into the arms of the silver sand beside the big blue bay
but in my heart I saw the proud black prow bursting the waves
as the flames waved farewell to your soaring spirit.

Next year I will go to the beach where our children played
fold a flotilla of paper boats (remember the story?)
wax night lights for cargo. Lit and launched at dusk
they will jewel the velvet sea until they burn and drown.

An Opener of the Way

...we need to remember that man's sojourn on this earth, due to the fragile covering of his outer physical body, is only a very short one indeed. In truth, considering man's noble soul, it is a short road for man to travel. Man's life on this earth cannot be for very long. It is necessary, and it has been decreed, that man on this earth must experience death.

Thus, in reality, man's life on this earth does not conform to God's creation of him as an excellent, noble creature. However, if the truth of the situation can be known or received, man's death on this earth is really a true blessing for him. For through death, man can rise up or change in state, so that he goes on until he comes to the place where he should be. But someone who is unable to understand and be aware of the true human life that is in his soul, will meet with darkness in the way of his true destination as willed by the One who creates, that is, the One God.

In truth, it is not God's will for man to be given life and created on this earth only to die and only to meet with darkness, with no true direction from his human soul. It is therefore necessary for man to survey and try somehow to find the true path, his true human state, so that death, which is always appointed for man, will be like the opening of the way for him to continue his true life in the direction willed by God. Clearly, man's death is an opener of the way, or an open gate, for him to be able to continue his life.

Bapak
London, England
November 29, 1957

FRIENDS

A FRIEND'S SUICIDE

~ ANONYMOUS

I was heartbroken when my 26 year old non-Subud friend committed suicide. The last time we'd spoken I'd wanted so much to give him a hug, but for some reason didn't.

Then one night I had an out-of-body experience. My soul went to where he was. It was reddish and many people were there. A couple that had died the same night he did was there too – a young man who, in a jealous rage, had shot his girlfriend and then himself, not far from where I lived. They were with him, but not really. He had a spirit guide, an old lady with long grey hair. Then he saw me and turned into an older man, then back to his younger self. I could see that there was no age in this place, just souls who had lost their way. I asked his forgiveness and then he said "Don't give up on the next one," and I said there was no-one else in my life. Then he said "There will be." What a gift he gave me that night. We embraced and in a split second he was torn away from me. Like something out of a movie. We were ripped apart, and I knew that was the end of our brief encounter, but at least I gave him that hug I had wanted to give him the last time we spoke.

I do look forward to the possibility of our paths crossing again some day; at least I am praying so... perhaps in God's vast, forgiving Heaven.

From *Reminders of Reality*

NO SMELL OF COFFEE

~ LAURIE LATHROP

David was a long time friend of our family. He always stayed in touch, and when life circumstances changed he would always come back and be with us for a while to regroup. So he was in and out of our lives for many years. At one time when he was with us he made wooden toys on machines in the basement. He taught my children and me how to finish the toys, and we accompanied him to craft fairs to help him sell his wares. He brought lightness and laughter into our home.

The last time he came home was following a grueling trip he had taken in search of his deepest inner Self. Although the trip was a success in that sense, it left him physically thin and weak, and it took him a long time to fully recuperate. This was in part because he had been managing diabetes for a long time without medication, staving off the worst of its effects with exercise and diet. He finally found a job that was meaningful to him, working with street kids as a probation officer for the state. Being able to help these troubled youth was important to him since he had himself had grown up on the streets of New York. As government budgets became tight, his case load increased, and his sense of how useful he could be was no longer clear. During this time his stepson had a fatal kayaking accident that deeply affected him. Ultimately, he resigned from his work.

David was an active member of Subud for many years, and after the debilitating trip he seldom missed a latihan. Following his resignation he had time to practice the latihan by himself and to read. Some serious health issues went untreated after he stopped working due to cost, including diabetes. After a few months it was clear he was not well, but he never complained.

Each morning he would go up to the kitchen to make coffee and take it back to his basement home and workshop. It was such an everyday routine: I could smell the aroma and know that all was well. But one morning there was no basement door opening, no sounds of making coffee, and no aroma. That made me wonder: "Is he all right? Should I go downstairs to see how he is doing?" I felt not to bother him. But I sensed that something was different.

A couple of hours later I asked again, "Should I go downstairs and check on him?"

No, not at this time.

Several more times I asked, and always felt "Not yet."

As the day passed I felt more and more strongly that he was going through a process that should not be interrupted. He had always been very clear that if he were ever in a diabetic coma or unconscious for any reason, he did not want to be resuscitated. This was a little different; the sense of process was more and more clear.

About 5:00 in the afternoon I felt, "Yes, it's all right to go down now." At first I couldn't find him, but then I saw him lying in the floor near his bed. His eyes were closed and his chest wasn't moving. He looked relaxed and peaceful. I felt it was time to make the necessary calls. It had never before occurred to me before that death might not be abrupt but rather an internal process that could take all day.

All the things that needed to be settled fell into place smoothly, with grace and ease. My daughter and I took some of his ashes to his birthplace, Puerto Rico, and released them into the sea as he had wished.

LOOKING AT THE OCEAN

~ MANUEL OLIVER

I had a friend who was dying and knew it. On what would be his last birthday, we drove an hour from our little village to a town so that we could have an adventure. We went to a honky-tonk bar and listened to a loud rock band while playing cribbage and sipping cokes. It felt very quiet on the long drive home, poignant. That was the last time I can remember spending with him. A couple weeks later, I had driven to California with some other friends to escape the cold winter. We finally reached the Pacific Coast at Half Moon Bay, 20 miles south of San Francisco. That day we meandered down the coastal highway, stopping every so often to run on the beach or find a good place to picnic.

A couple hours before sunset, I found myself staring at the water and unable to think of anything but my old friend. I thought I saw him there, or imagined that I saw him, visiting me, getting one last look at the ocean in Santa Cruz where he had lived some of the happiest times of his life. I remember thinking that he was looking at the ocean vicariously through me, one last time.

A couple hours after this experience, I was able to get to a phone, call back home and confirm that he had, in fact, died that day.

MY FRIEND JO

~ ADRIENNE THOMAS

Death and dying is all around us. Here in Lewes is a project called Living Well, Dying well which is working hard to change attitudes to this greatest taboo. Meanwhile, my friends are leaving, mainly through cancer, and their deaths have been a profound experience for me, as they each died "consciously".

I'll talk about just one of those deaths, as it is the most recent and still very raw. Jo was a unique person. She had a profoundly difficult childhood which left her unable to easily form relationships. She could be very challenging, but offered friendship at a very deep and insightful level... no small talk or frivolity. She could also be great fun.

She came to see me straight after her diagnosis of aggressive breast cancer. She said, "I don't mind dying but I do regret that I've never really lived." That was Jo. She went through the whole routine of aggressive chemo, which was horrible to witness. She lived alone and we formed a support group around her, taking in food, helping with cleaning etc. She had surgery which was less traumatic and then seemed to recover remarkably well.

She had a two year period of energy and creativity, marked only occasionally with the depression which had haunted her for much of her life.

Then she suddenly developed symptoms of breathlessness which worsened over a few weeks. Doctors were saying she had low blood pressure but she could hardly walk and eventually her mother took her to A+E and insisted they check her out.

She was on oxygen and morphine within her first 24 hours there, so deep down I knew it was bad. She called me one morning and said, "It's not good. There are holes in my bones."

She was transferred to a beautiful room in our local hospice and within four weeks, she was dead. She was 56 years old.

We were and still are all shocked and grieving, yet there was so much that was positive. Jo had lived a childhood with two narcissistic parents who basically left her to fend for herself. She never felt loved. She died surrounded by the kind of love and care she could only ever have dreamed of. My good friend Annabella and I were left exhausted, trying to keep down the number of visitors who wanted to be with her, and take care of her. I was massaging her feet one day when she suddenly opened her eyes and looked directly at me and smiled. I felt immediately that she was in exactly the right place and that this was all exactly how it should be... her death was in the order of things.

Jo had only recently been opened in Subud and she found great comfort in this dimension of her busy life as a therapist. Once, when latihaning with her during her illness, I felt this tremendous "energy body" within her physical body. Bright blue in colour, it was full of life and energy and complete, down to the fingers and toes. I then felt the outer body as a mere shell to be easily sloughed off, like a thin, brittle outer skin.

As deaths go, Jo's was a good death, peaceful, quick and full of love.

REMEMBERING RIDWAN

~ LILLIANA GIBBS

One year ago, on March 6, Ridwan Russ died in a car accident near Melbourne, Australia. He was 28.

The eldest son of Halimah and Alhazmi, Ridwan was brother to Alexandra and Magnus. Thirty years ago I was an attendant at Muchsin (as he was known then) and Halimah's wedding in Cilandak. We have known each other in differing circumstances over the years, and Halimah is my closest friend.

When I got the call, I went to Melbourne. Alhazmi and Magnus – then living in Brisbane– and Alexandra from London, had just arrived. Halimah's mother Joan came from Perth, and Utami, wife of her brother Mansur, came from Indonesia. It was an extraordinary time, and I wrote about it to Mansur who had been visiting Canada.

On this first anniversary of Ridwan's death, I felt I wanted to share the experience more broadly.

Alhazmi had expressed the significant obligation he felt to wash Ridwan's body. But after attempts to organise this with other men in the traditional Muslim way, it became clear that Alhazmi would need our help.

And so it was that Ridwan was lovingly washed and prepared by his father, his sister, his aunt and friend, in what was an extraordinary process for each of us.

We were fortunate that the funeral people supported us completely– sensitive to our need to be alone, and being on hand as needed.

I felt prepared and willing for what we had come to do, but it was still a shock to see Ridwan's naked body so completely without life. To stand beside his father and sister as they witnessed this reality was achingly painful. It was so beyond what is ordinary, I felt on the edge of being lost, and of surrendering, and looked to Utami. We so needed each other to be present for Alhazmi and Alexandra– and together we became strong, sister pillars.

The latihan was a powerful presence. We sang and cried and prayed as we gently cleaned Ridwan's body, and washed his hair. Utami provided the Islamic form, giving a pattern for Alhazmi to follow – first rinse the head three times, then the right side, then the left.

The experience of washing Ridwan was so powerful, and in the end the difference was palpable. We witnessed the transformation of a young, broken body to a beautiful, peaceful being, wrapped in rose petals and white cloth, ready for burial. I was filled with the sense that everything was done just as it should have been – confirmed by the contentment on Alexandra's and Alhazmi's faces.

When we went outside we were amazed that it was many hours later... time had bent into another shape altogether.

Ridwan's funeral was a loving community event that filled the church. Friends carried his coffin, and a beautiful young opera singer's voice expressed exquisite joy and anguish.

Love and support flowed from every direction. Flowers filled the house, food parcels and meals arrived as needed, money and messages came from the Subud community worldwide, and from friends everywhere; Ridwan's workmates, acquaintances, friends, parents and friends.

When I left to return home to Sydney a week later, I felt I was stepping out of a protective bubble that had surrounded us all. In Halimah and Alhazmi I saw such courage and surrender – each in their own way very much living the whole experience –the shock, the blessings, the tears, the love, and pain. Able to be open to all that had happened, and was happening. For each of them, and Magnus and Alexandra, there was a long journey still ahead.

It was a special time and I am so grateful that I could have been of service.

With love, Lilliana

My first experience of death was when Ibu died in Cilandak in 1971. I was 13 years old, and was included with all the women who came to wash her body. Under a canopy of batik on the roof garden of Bapak's house, women sang and cried and lovingly bathed Ibu for the last time. I remember the heat, the scent of frangipani and rosewater, and the beautiful feeling. It was this experience that gave me the understanding and the courage to help prepare Ridwan's body.

UNANSWERED QUESTION

~ STEPHANIE FERRERIA

Vardi, one of our Subud sisters, had died and we went to wash her body and wrap it in a white sheet. We did latihan afterwards for her and I received the image of water with drops of water entering the pool and becoming part of the pool.

Then something energetically entered my third eye. It was a weird sensation, almost like it had a sound of boring.

Well, I went off to a gathering not long thereafter, and people were invited to ask a question of their guru. I asked the lady what she thought the experience of the third eye was all about. She said that when someone dies, they can pass on some trait that they have really honed in their life on to someone else. I have wondered if that is truly what that experience was, and if so, what sort of ability I was given.

ANIMAL SIGHTINGS

~ ELNA KELLY

It was Valentine's week this year. I was driving home about 7 o'clock one evening in my neighborhood when I saw a giant raccoon crossing the street. I slowed down, rolled down the window and said to the raccoon, "Be careful!"

All that weekend I was really sad, without knowing why. I was crying tears as I drove.

Monday was a school holiday. I woke up early and drove to the beach. I found a beautiful heart-shaped stone. When I held it I felt calm.

As I was driving home I saw a coyote crossing the road. I was thinking: "Animal sightings... What does this mean? I should google it!"

I was preparing dinner for my nephew and his girlfriend when I got a phone call from my childhood friend Mary. She told me that Gregory Webster, whom I had known for forty-five years, had died on Valentine's Day. The sadness in my heart that I had been feeling, and the strange animal sightings I'd had... It all made sense. To me it was proof that we know and feel things that we are not aware of cognitively.

COLORED LIGHTS

~ REYNOLD WEISSINGER

Sometimes I have an experience after a brother dies, usually in the context of a dream. When this happens, the feeling is of a more intense reality, rather than a dream. Today I was thinking of Mas Prio. Before his death we were working on something together. And there were times we felt very close. At a difficult time he was very generous to me. So I felt sorrow when he died. Perhaps more sorrow than I knew. The dream about Prio came shortly after he died. I was looking for him in a large old hotel, similar to the Miramar where Bapak stayed in Los Angeles. I entered one of the large ballrooms, and immediately felt his presence. But it was dark and I couldn't see him. I walked around the room, and soon saw some lights that seemed to float in the air. They were different colors, and were moving energetically in circular patterns. As I drew close I realized, That's Prio! And I opened my arms to embrace him. But the lights entered my chest, and I felt the energy of a powerful latihan.

Ready to Go

It is when at the moment of forgetfulness we are reminded. That is the meaning of iman. And that is actually the most important thing in our life because it is that which will be present at the moment when we are facing our death.

At the moment when we face our death we are usually in a state of forgetfulness. We forget everything, even our children, our families, our life in this world. But at that moment we will have the consciousness of life still there within us. And this is why, if this is really present within someone, then at the moment when he is about to die, and he has forgotten everything, at that moment he is able to say the name of Almighty God.

There have been many Subud members that have already experienced this. And Bapak wants to tell you one. Bapak specifically chooses someone who is not an Indonesian but an experience of a Subud member which happened outside of Indonesia so that you feel it is not so far away from you.

Our brother Edward Van Hein, Bapak was told this story by his family. Actually Edward was completely fine. There was nothing wrong with him. He was just sitting one evening with his wife and his daughter, I think, and he just said to them at one moment, he said, "Just a moment. You stay here and go on talking. I have something very important to do." And he went upstairs to his room.

So they didn't pay any attention. He went into his room and he locked his door. And it seems (because, of course, nobody witnessed it) that he then lay down on his bed and at that moment he died. In other words, he left this world. And Bapak can tell you that he went up, upwards at that moment.

After a long time his wife and his daughter, who were sitting downstairs began to wonder what Edward was doing, why he hadn't come down again.

So they finally went upstairs and they tried to open the door and found it was locked, and they couldn't get any answer. Finally they opened the door by force and found Edward lying on his bed with his hands folded on his chest.

They quickly called the doctor and raised the alarm, as it were. And, of course, the doctor, being an ordinary human doctor who is only aware of this world, became suspicious. How come he wasn't called before when Edward was sick? How come he's only called when Edward is lying on his bed all neatly laid out? Naturally a suspicion arose in his mind. Has he been poisoned by his family? Or has this or that happened?

So he ordered an autopsy. But, of course, when they performed the autopsy it showed that he didn't die of anything in particular.

This is a real experience, Bapak said. It shows a way of dying that can take place if it is already truly guided by the Power of Almighty God. There are many instances of this.

> Bapak
> Hoboken, NJ U.S.A.
> July 4, 1981

ANCESTORS

REMEMBERING OUR FOREBEARS

~ LEONARD HITCHCOCK

As a child I suffered with asthma but gradually improved as I grew older though never being completely free of it.

There was a period in the late 1980s when it suddenly came back quite severely. The unusual element this time was that it used to develop in the evening, became quite severe during the night but then eased off as it got light. I would say that this lasted for a period of about four weeks and I was getting little sleep. However I felt very clearly that this was a purification illness and that I shouldn't seek medical help. This was also confirmed by the fact that as the asthma got worse with the darkening day, inwardly I experienced a corresponding feeling of elation or joy which was present all the time I was suffering with the asthma. This was also a proof for me that this was a very beneficial process that was happening.

On this particular night I had been asleep and woke up in bed in the early hours. I was completely unable to breathe at all; my lungs were unable to function because of the very severe asthma and I knew that I was going to die. I felt completely calm and relaxed about this – actually I was totally indifferent! Whether I lived or died at that point seemed to me to be completely and utterly inconsequential – of no importance one way or the other.

The next thing I experienced was being in a vast space surrounded by golden light and I was in the centre of a circle of people. I knew that these were people whom I was close to although I could not make out individual faces or people. I experienced what I can only describe as a 'wave of love' emanating from everyone which was carrying and supporting me – it was the most wonderful sensation!

The next that I knew was wakening up in the morning from a deep and restful sleep. I understand from later experiences that these people were actually my relatives who had passed on. This experience has left me with a profound gratitude towards these ancestors who have shaped my life in this world and we should remember that our forebears have passed on blessings to us as well as burdens!!

There is a follow-up story to this one that occurred many years later in 2009.

Shortly after my father's death I contracted a severe lung infection which turned into pneumonia. At this point I should say that I had always been of the opinion that my lung weakness had been inherited from my paternal grandfather who had contracted lung cancer [and indeed only had one lung during the period I knew him].

One night during this illness [before it had developed into pneumonia] I was sitting quietly and became aware of a presence. I understood that this was my mother's father whom I had never known [he died when my mother was a young girl]. I understood that he was very pleased to be with me and there was a very loving feeling from him. At this point I inwardly heard my mother telling me that her father had died of pneumonia – something that I had completely forgotten about – and I understood at this point that my lung weakness was actually a purification of her side of the family.

I then had a long 'conversation' with my grandfather. He told me that he had met me once before and I recalled the incident described above with the bad asthma when I nearly died. He told me that he had been there in that golden space. He also gave me an insight into the nature of the 'illness' or purification that I was undergoing and in particular the emotional and psychological patterns or tendencies associated with it – because illness actually manifests at all levels of being but often we're only aware of the physical. I was shown certain tendencies in my nature or character associated with this illness and which needed to be cleaned. This was very helpful and I really understood for the first time that our inner development has to include all our forebears as well. He also gave me some practical instructions about posture and breathing.

This sounds strange but during the experience it actually felt very normal. I should also add that I was aware that he had a very profound feeling of gratitude for the grace of the Latihan.

One evening I was doing a Latihan at home with a very close Subud brother – it was actually very late and during the period known as the 'Month of the Ancestors' – the month preceding Ramadan.

This particular Latihan was very deep and powerful and at a certain point I knew I had reached a place which I call the boundary of this world and the next. I was then told from within '*now* you can pray for your ancestors'.

From this I understood that for our prayers to be relevant or true it was necessary to be at this point or state of surrender inwardly.

BLUE AND RED ROADS

~ ANONYMOUS

I had read that as a Subud member my latihan would affect my ancestors for seven generations back. Other than being greeted by images of European looking people in a latihan shortly after I was opened, I didn't really have much of an idea of what that meant – not, that is, until my paternal grandmother died. Upon my grandmother's death, I found out that I had a whole bunch of ancestors that I was clueless about.

My father has always told me that we can tell that we have Native American ancestry because we have orange earwax, and other earwax is golden. I haven't checked people's earwax to find out if this is the case, but in any event my dad and aunt look Native American. Their manner has a quality that feels Native American. They've always lived close to the land and love it in a way that is precious to me. I have felt a kinship with Native American values on the inside, but on the outside I look to be a fair-skinned European. The only thing that distinguishes me from the blue-eyed redheads and blondes of my mother's side of the family is that I have my father's dark, straight hair and my eyes are hazel.

My father's side of the family is interested in genealogy and they know a lot about everyone except my great grandfather, who is the big family secret. My great grandfather is said to have been full-blooded Native American and conceived a child out-of-wedlock with my great grandmother. Because the child was born out-of-wedlock, the married sister raised the child. No one knows the name or the tribal heritage of the Native American great grandfather. If this story is accurate, I would presumably be $1/8^{th}$ American Indian and $7/8^{th}$ Northern European. In any event, *I was soon to discover that it didn't really matter that I had no clue about my American Indian ancestors. They knew me.* So here is how this discovery came about.

My husband picks up the phone one evening and hears in a casual conversational tone the words, "Well, she packed it in about six o'clock." My husband makes the brilliant guess that it is probably my father's voice and that someone has died. I phone my dad and I agree to fly out and sing "Amazing Grace" in harmony with my two aunts for my grandmother's funeral. I then phone my Subud sisters to request a latihan on behalf of my grandmother, as is the custom at our Subud center. The next evening, we are gathered to do a latihan on behalf of my grandmother. The word "begin" is barely spoken, and boom, I am down on my knees bowing and chanting in some American Indian tongue. I feel the gentleness of my grandmother's spirit. Afterwards, a sister comments that my grandmother can go anywhere she wants.

I contract some sort of flu on the plane and arrive at the farmhouse of relatives that I have not seen in twenty years. At this moment of reunion, I throw up on the lawn. Fortunately, a medical doctor and three nurses are inside, and they happily greet me and swipe my wrist with some magical drug that takes away my nausea. Their manner is so casual and cheerful. A little stomach flu is nothing to fuss about. I am in the nest of my kin.

The next day, thanks to a little swipe on my wrist of the miracle drug, I sing "Amazing Grace" in three-part harmony with my aunts at my grandmother's funeral. Draped over my grandmother's casket is a large white afghan, in which she had crocheted the Lord's Prayer in perfect stitches. The blue ribbon that came with the white baby blanket that she sent at our daughter's birth meant that the blanket had won first prize at the County Fair. My sister-in-law says that she has stored enough of those white baby blankets that my grandmother crocheted that she can supply future generations too. I recall that Bapak had said that we receive the latihan if we have an ancestor who truly worshipped God. I suspect that I received the latihan because of this grandmother.

Upon my return home, my latihans continue with the Native American theme. I chant in deep tones. I have latihans around various Native American people's experiences. I write down some of the words that I speak and chant in latihan. I search on the internet, and I get some matches with Shoshone. I test with a helper and she receives that I have American Indian ancestry from several tribes.

One evening, I am standing in latihan in a state of deep, luscious peace. An American Indian man holding a large medicine shield with four feathers draping down from it stands above me to one side. Golden light pours through the medicine shield into me. Throughout the whole latihan, light pours into me from the medicine shield.

The next day, I meet with an acquaintance that has some psychic abilities. He comments to me, "You have an eagle in golden light on your forehead". He has no knowledge of my personal life or Subud experiences. He makes another comment which happens to be accurate, which is that I should get the tires changed on my car. I can't see anything on my forehead.

On another day, I am at the carwash, and one of the workers looks towards me and comments to another worker, "Creo que es una águila porque es muy grande." Translated that means, "I think she is an eagle because she is very big." Physically, I am rather small of stature, so, once again, someone is seeing something that is not visible to me.

I wish I knew something about what these latihans mean. I test with a helper and she receives that the shaman was someone that my ancestors worshipped and my ancestors sent him on my behalf. Wow! My ancestors know me and are looking after me.

The Native American latihans continue. On one evening I experience being shot by an arrow. I feel the arrow go right into my chest. On another evening, I see an entire family laid out in white ceremonial calf-skin robes. They are all dead, including the children. I cry and cry. I seem to be processing traumatic events that happened to people.

The Native American chanting during latihan causes an expansion of my vocal range. Normally, I am a soprano. Now my vocal range extends to a complete octave below middle C. I guess this is one of those unexpected perks from being steadfast in attending latihan.

One day a helper receives that God would like me to pray "for my ancestors to be forgiven back to the beginning of my line." How far is back to the beginning of my line? What have I or my ancestors done to deserve such generosity? I take on a larger role in Subud, and so I feel like I am giving back enough to make the prayer. One day I pray for my ancestors to be forgiven back to the beginning of my line while driving to visit a Subud sister. When I arrive, she says, "Your ancestors are here. They are singing." More specifically, my Native American ancestors are chanting.

Eventually, after two years, the Native American latihans stopped and the content of my latihan changed. Perhaps someday when I "pack it in" and go home, I'll get to meet them. If they are anything like my kin on the good red road, they'll be friendly and not care one whit how I show up. I'll be welcomed, and of course, there will be singing, maybe on both the blue and red roads.

From *Reminders of Reality*

CHILDREN

DELIVERANCE
FOR HAITI, JANUARY 10, 2010

~ RASUNAH KATZ

Does the name define the body?
the soul?
Who is the *I* then?
When the little one cries out,
Mama, please do not let me die
We hear the words as though they are ours,
we are the ones buried there,
not those bright calm eyes looking back.

Didn't this already happen?
Wasn't Katrina enough?
Was she her name?
Was the cement solid?
Was her terror ours?
Is the *I* dissolving?
Are we all victims of a fate
that cannot be changed?

Not by a name
Not by choosing a different path
Not by all the victims calling out once
Nothing can change the babies who live
from those who die.
Was this necessary?
If you tell me it was,
I will not believe you.
I will call you a false prophet.
I will say to abandon hope is to change reality.
If you saw her belief,

her tremendous courage,
the endearing braids crusted with dust
you would say, *I am changed.*
You would say that this great upheaval,
this loss, is life as it presents itself.

And that child, all the children who suffer
are one heart exposed.
We cannot be spared their suffering,
we can only concentrate,
we can only labour,
we can only cry out with them,
Have mercy,
until it is over.

It is in this
exceptional moment
of notice,
of witness,
that we are surrendered
delivered by those souls
transforming
creation itself.

SANDY HOOK

~ EMMANUEL WILLIAMS

Children were out there
trapped in a nowhere place.
That's what they told me.
I saw leaves on a flowing of water
caught by a rock or a branch
tugging and stuck.

I didn't know who they were
the ones who were telling me this
but I trusted them.
They said the children were screaming
There was fear all over them
Such fear they said,
as we have rarely witnessed
tearing and crackling all over them
and inside them

I could hardly bear to listen to them
but they wanted to tell me
because I love children.

The children were all wounded
they said
such terrible wounds on them

I saw mouths gaping and screaming
I saw holes, like eyes staring into the dark

wounds still bleeding
they said
though their bodies were back down there.

My heart was in such pain

We went to them, they said
we gathered them
we held each little one warm and safe
we summoned light and love
we touched the wounds and healed them

Their pain.
We opened. We were drawing their pain into our beings
their fear and their pain
They were no longer screaming
Their sobs still shook them
the loss of all they knew and loved still hurt and hurt and hurt

I sat for a long time with my eyes closed
I was listening

They said
The children are here with us.
We will care for them
until they are ready to go on

They asked me to tell you this.

AIDS

~ CHELLIE KEW

Through her eyes
I am touched by grace

This small child's gaze
dark as ink wells,
draws me into her soul.
An old soul
compassion emanating,
many lifetimes has she borne witness to.

She carries her tiny frame
wrapped around the core of her spiritual beliefs,
illumination;
a cross centered
holds her body in its rightful place.

I am in the presence of God.

I sense a knowing gratitude,
courage given for this mission
I am about to embark on.

She may well die this day
or the next.
Peace rests in her face
resolution
for she knows she shall return
into the waiting arms of her maker

TAKING MY BABY TO HEAVEN

~ AMELIA WILLIAMS

When I was very young, before I knew about God and my soul, I was pregnant. Unable to embrace this life change I did what others had done before me. I never felt good about this, even if I didn't feel exactly 'wrong'. But I did eventually learn to ask forgiveness and pray for the soul of the life that I had carried so fleetingly.

Many many years later I was finally able to receive the birth of our daughter. It was a time of long awaited joy. But during the first few months I began to sense a presence that became gently persistent. I started to suspect and feel that this was unfinished business of my earlier pregnancy.

Testing confirmed that the soul of this departed child was still near. I asked her what she wanted or what she needed. She explained that when I terminated the pregnancy she and I had made an agreement. She would stay with me until my own child came. She would stay with me because she loved me and because she herself would benefit from this connection. The agreement was that I would release her when the time came. But... I had 'forgotten' this promise. Now she needed to leave and she required my assistance to release her.

First she needed to be held and rocked and cuddled for the infant she was. This was a deeply loving exchange for us both, as I held her in my spirit arms. Then we began to... travel. We journeyed for some time beyond any reality that I have known then or since, beyond the world, beyond landmarks, beyond knowing. It was a seamless glide toward the eternal, and we were as one – until I was stopped. "This is as far as you can go" came the gentle whisper of the guardian who met us at the threshold, and I understood that this journey was not mine to complete. As I lifted the babe, she was enfolded by arms of eternal love, whisked away, and suddenly I was 'home.'

I have never since felt her presence, yet the imprint of her love is forever with me.

MULTIPLES

DANELLA'S STORY

~ DANELLA MAUGUIN

I still can hear his voice quietly saying, "I received I will die on Friday." My mind raced. It was a Wednesday morning in late June 2012. I was in Sacramento and he was hospitalized in San Francisco. I was beyond exhausted and driving two hours was out of the question. I felt the adrenalin flow through my body and intense emotion engulf me. I let the emotion take over, no holding back on this one. I wanted Ibrahim to know how much I cared for him, difficult as he sometimes was. "Don't go. Don't go. Hold on. I'm coming tomorrow." I pleaded. I must have repeated this three or four times, tears soaking my cheeks. I knew he could "ask" to wait and his request just, just may be granted. I asked him to "ask". The thought of him leaving without me being with him at the moment of his death was unthinkable. It was against the plan. I was to be at his side when he died. A dear friend unselfishly offered to drive me to the hospital in San Francisco. We left the following morning.

For him, accepting that he was going to die sooner rather than later was an accomplishment. Once he was told his end was days away, he stopped fighting. Cool acceptance took over, at least on the outer. Finding himself still alive on Saturday morning, he playfully said to me, "This dying business is difficult." He so wanted to live and did all he could to make this happen. Ibrahim believed in persisting. And persist he did. What lawyer doesn't?

When I arrived at the hospital the next day, his room was filled with friends from Subud, A.A. and Alanon. He had phoned everyone asking them to, "Come say your goodbyes." They came. His sons from Los Angeles, his "Darling baby daughter" arrived from India with her family, his estranged sister from the East Coast. His personal friend, the head of cardiology at UCSF sat by his bedside and they talked. Ibrahim's beloved oncologist spoke to him on the phone. He was surrounded by people who loved and respected him, warts and all. I remember him saying with surprise and sincere gratitude in his voice, "I am surrounded by such love." "Yes you are, my love." I remained with him in the hospital, sleeping next to his bed the last nine days of his life.

Ibrahim's actual passing did take place on a Friday, although a week later. He hadn't received which Friday, just Friday. On Friday, July 6, 2012 at about 11:47-11:49am he passed. His daughter was on his right side, singing in his ear and I was on the left, stroking his forehead and whispering, "My love, my love" in his ear. Others surrounded his bed which was now facing east in the Islamic tradition.

Thursday was a difficult, a very difficult night for Ibrahim. I awoke that Friday morning knowing he would not last until noon. And he left before then. I was intent on making the outer aspects of his death as peaceful for him as possible. His final spiritual preparation was between Ibrahim and God. This was not my territory. And his outer surroundings were just as important as his physical comfort. Nothing was to interrupt the process. I needed help. Little did I know there was help at hand. Frequently in Subud when there is a real need, the need gets satisfied. Our job is to "pay attention" and then follow with action. He certainly did.

I was overtired and emotional. Keeping constant watch, I hadn't really slept for nine days. That morning a young L.P.N., overhearing my distraught phone conversation with a Subud sister, approached me saying, "I am a practicing Muslim. Would you like me to recite the prayers to Mr. Butler?" He hadn't spoken in days and our signal for "Yes" was him opening his eyes. When I asked Ibrahim if he wanted to hear a recitation of the prayers, those eyes of his opened wide, very wide. Although close to death, he was alert and aware of his surroundings. It was a "Yes!" She chanted the prayers in Arabic. I could see him smile. Then another surprise. "Would Mr. Butler like his bed to be facing east?" The nursing home attendants were there in a flash. I asked for and was immediately given a clean, smooth white pillowcase to cover his face when the moment came. Doing this was very important to me. He was to have every Islamic observance I could supply. All was ready. His darling daughter arrived at 10:50am. The vigil quietly began.

The actual moment of Ibrahim's soul leaving his body was almost imperceptible, so subtle was his departure. What I personally witnessed was his soul departing before his physical body died. There was a minute or two in difference between these events. Officially, the pronouncement of a person's death is when the actual physical body stops; there is no pulse. Often the soul departs before the body ceases. Upon witnessing his demise I felt a combination of relief, sorrow and grief. Relief for Ibrahim; his physical suffering had finished. He was now on his way. And my own personal grief at losing "My Love." The love that came to me late in my own life.

Now almost two years later I remain grateful.

HANIA'S STORY

~ HANI'A HUMMINGBIRD HOTOTO

Like many people, I had an underlying fear and anxiety concerning the mystery of death. I remember the realization of the inevitable taking root in my psyche as an adolescent, and it affected me so that for a while I became afraid of the dark just as I has been as a child. During this anxiety spell about death, I even became afraid of going to sleep, for as I lay down I'd hear my heart beat and rushing blood in my ears, and was afraid I would hear the beating of my heart stop and know I'd be dead; whatever that meant. To my embarrassment, this anxiety about death would recur from time to time even in my teens and early adult-hood. Fortunately, for my being able to function in life, much time would elapse between these bouts with anxiety about death, and I would forget that I had them until they would unexpectedly appear again, for a night or two, or even a whole week. I always kept these episodes a secret.

Well into adulthood, these anxiety spells about death became less intense and I became able to ignore them when they appeared. I no longer lost any sleep, but the unresolved mystery of death would haunt me until sleep came. I'm happy to relate I no longer have any anxiety about death, and for this I have Ibrahim Butler to thank...

Were it not for Subud, I doubt I'd ever have become friends with Ibrahim Butler. We had nothing but the latihan in common; but then the latihan is the most important thing one can have in common with another! He had been in Subud many years, and I was new to the brotherhood. As some who knew him may remember, Ibrahim had a 'certain something' in his personality that could be a bit 'chafing'. It seems to me, as I search through my memory of how/why we became friends, that because I was not put off by this colorful aspect of his personality, Ibrahim took a liking to me, and because I would listen, and liked to listen, began to share with me many of his Subud anecdotes and adventures. And because it fell to me during a California congress to stay up all night and keep watch over him as he slept for his blood pressure had become dangerously low, Ibrahim naturally felt very grateful towards me for having done so, and the seed of our friendship was sown.

Brother Ibrahim had been battling cancer for some time before we became friends, along with diabetes and other ailments, and his health took a turn for the worse after a fall that necessitated him having a hip replacement. This occurred at a time when, in my latihan, I was asking to be shown a feeling of brotherhood, beyond the ordinary flaky brotherhood of my selfish heart/mind, and which I began to spontaneously wish for out of my appreciation for this Gift from God that we have been so fortunate to receive. I learned that when one asks God for something concerning one's growth and understanding, one way God grants it is to present one with an opportunity to act: an opportunity to live and experience directly an event through which one is taught; one has to step up and show up and do what the event requires of one.

God teaches through such experience; and it can happen you get more than you asked for!

So, through his recuperation from his hip surgery I'd visit Ibrahim in the hospital, and against recommendations and doctor's orders, sneak him his beloved Peet's coffee, for which he was very appreciative and which solidified our bond as brothers and friends. Ibrahim recovered well enough from his hip surgery, and I'd visit him at his home and help with things around the house that he could no longer do. I got to see a side of Ibrahim perhaps not many have seen: at the same Cal congress, he had become smitten with Danella M., and she with him and they became 'special friends'. It was an entertaining privilege for me to witness their love for one another, and though they were quite mature about it all, they still had the freshness of young folks underneath; but sooner than we would have liked, his illness surged and he was hospitalized again. I visited him when I could, and he appreciated much my coming to see him, and even during the later stages, when he was very weak, Brother Ibrahim would let me know he loved and appreciated me by opening his eyes to see me and squeezing my hand, which sometimes seemed to take all the strength he could muster.

Now, I must confess that at first I had to struggle a bit to visit Ibrahim, because like I said we hadn't anything of ordinary life in common, and, well: we all know how the material world can present us with all sorts of 'better things to do'. But I'd remember my wish, that I'd asked God to be shown a feeling of brotherhood, and even If I didn't feel like it, I'd muster a sense of duty and go bring brother Ibrahim a Peet's coffee. I am so glad I did so. Brother Ibrahim had somewhat strained relationships with some members of his family, who were in other parts of the country and world, and for a time Danella and I were his only bedside companions, Danella much more than me. She was his true bedside companion. But I wonderfully was able to witness the mending of his relationship with his sons, daughter, and sister, who rallied to his side when they learned his time on earth was coming to a close. I realized we all have flaws, weaknesses in ourselves that create strains in our relationships, but that underneath is an abiding love ever ready to blossom, and that unlike the blossoms of the trees of the Earth, the blossoming love within us never fades and dies.

Danella and I were present at his bedside when Brother Ibrahim left his body. The experience was profound for me. Ibrahim 'spoke' to me from the 'other side'. He told me to tell his family, especially his sister, who really needed to know, that he loved them, and that we all should love one another. Being able to comfort his sister with what Ibrahim told me was also profound for me, I realized I had an authenticity that was much more than the words I spoke. I realized also that I felt kin to her, and to everyone; even the nursing home staff. The whole experience was remarkable yet so ordinary; so: 'yep this is what it is and how it happens, no big deal', yet from what I experienced it is a Big Wonderful Deal! – Later I, along with another Subud brother, was doing latihan in the room with where Ibrahim's body was lying, and towards the end I actually felt Ibrahim looking down from above with Bapak at his side! I am so privileged to have had the experience!

And so, Allah granted me my wish in that unexpected way that God Almighty seems to like to do things: I got my understanding and real feeling/experience of Subud brotherhood, and as an added bonus: no more anxiety about death!

DYING BY DEGREES

~ KADARIJAH GARDINER

"Take your time,
Slow if you please
Take your time.
Take it with ease."

This song from my youth
Has wisdom yet,
And "yet" has wisdom too.
For time is running out
I felt it, I feel it through
My fingers' very fibre.

I enjoy the sound of his breathing
Beside me on the bed.
Exhausted he is by the shock
Of seeing me, feeling me, so near collapse.

I'll be still, with the weight of the tray on my knees,
But no weight in my heart,
Just the knowledge that I'm still here
That's weight enough, God knows.
Weight enough for me to sleep.

Reading Eliot's Little Gidding together
Was a link to live and a taste of heaven
Both world and sense linked.

My veins are in a sort of recovering shock still.
An odd feeling when I move, or if I don't.
I sense their independent life.

Are they wondering what's happened?
Did they think their work was done?
That they could "knock off" now?
But oh, I see is that why I am still to go on?
For if I start and went into the beyond,
They wouldn't. So they keep on working,
Always working for more than
Eighty years! Poor things, all of them
The veins, tissues, arteries, lungs heart and all of them,
I don't blame you for conking out occasionally
But you see, we will have to move on soon
So we had better (much better!) sort ourselves out
Now and get to our proper place, all of us
So we can really "go home" all of us, by
God Almighty Grace.

KADARIJAH'S 100${}^{\text{TH}}$ DAY

~ SHARIFIN GARDINER

Hello my love, it's now a 100 days!
We miss you so, each in our several ways
But yet I've felt your sweet and gentle touch.
And then you came to comfort me so much:
A whispered greeting in your voice so clear.
Some say, in dreams or latihan, that you appear
To them. One friend said it was completely real.
Yes, now it's time for many things to heal.

So journey onward to that blessed sphere

Where Grace is,

And there's nothing left to fear.

February 21, 2014

THE DEATH OF RACHMAN ULMER:

~ AMINAH HERRMAN, FAMILY & A FRIEND

AMINAH

PRELUDE

Each of my family members would have a slightly different story to tell as to the events I am about to share...This is my account of my husband, Rachman Ulmer's passing... We were married for 32 years. I give my best recollection here for you now.

Rachman's passing and the events leading up to it are still hard for me to grasp. Everything happened so fast and there was no time to do anything but hang on for the ride. From diagnoses to Rachman's passing was 4½ months.

Within a six month's window of time, our son had nearly died in a major motorcycle accident, my father died, Rachman's father died and Rachman was diagnosed with the most aggressive form of lung cancer. When the doctor delivered the diagnosis they told him to get his affairs in order. We couldn't believe it. We sat stunned in the hospital. We looked long and hard at each other. Finally I said to him, "It seems like the only way to get through this is to stay in the present moment". We made a silent pact to support one another through this journey. I was thoroughly exhausted from all that the previous months had been, caring for our son, not knowing if he would make it, living out of a suitcase.. and I asked from within, "How can I face this now? I have no strength." I really had no idea where I could find the energy to face all that would be required. And yet we could feel the powerful energy of the love from so many people.. I have never felt so in need of help as I did then.

Rachman received his diagnosis in California after visiting family and attending my father's memorial. Our son Gordon and daughter Helise drove us back to Texas to our home we had not seen in over 7 months since caring for our son after his accident. We stayed with my sister, Covita and brother in law, Christopher, while our house was being readied. They had hired a special cleaning service to take care of the 7 months of dust and make it safer for Rachman. We were taken care of by them for a week or so. It was my brother in law, Christopher who shaved Rachman's head as his hair started falling out from the first chemo treatment received while still in California. Our son Hamilton and our son in law, Isom, did a great deal to prepare the house for our arrival. It was good to have our family around us. My sister, brother in law and our children rallied around us with loving urgency. There were a lot of anxious, hopeful thoughts that we might find a way to prolong Rachman's time. A great deal of research into his illness was done, new protocols, alternative practices etc. Rachman was received into a county program and was able to begin subsequent chemo treatments which we were told might extend his life but not cure it. The county plan was not smooth. The treatments rooms were lined up with people...you took a number to wait your turn for chemo. The rooms were grey and hard. And yet we both kept feeling that a way was being made for us to navigate through all the difficulties. Rachman had an enormous amount of courage and faced his illness with dignity.

RACHMAN'S JOURNEY

Rachman and I entered what I think of now as a "sacred space". The time of day, the outer circumstances, none of this mattered any more. We seem to have a shared inner understanding: "We're doing this together" – words that were known but never said. Every decision, every challenge, every problem was felt and resolved in that sacred space, and nothing seemed to throw it off – we felt we were in a protective bubble. We could feel unseen help.

At first, when Rachman was diagnosed as having lung cancer, I was intent on finding ways to prolong his life, to do it right, to give him maybe five more years, to give him time. I spent a lot of energy considering all kinds of suggestions – alternative remedies of all kinds. Someone sent us special herbal tincture made with special healing herbs from Russia. Someone sent remedies intended to slow down the proliferation of the cells. We were sent so many remedies known to help stave off cancer. We had piles of them on the table... We listed them all and took the list to have them checked by the doctor. The kind prayers of many people lifted our spirits. It also was a medicine to soothe the difficulties.

Then after a Rachman's fourth chemo treatment we were told that it hadn't worked and that the cancer had spread by another 20%. Rachman was not surprised. "I've done this to myself" he said. "I have only myself to blame." He never blamed anyone. He accepted the reality of his prognosis. He faced it directly, clearly, with resolve.

We called hospice and were given a team of very caring people. By a stroke of unbelievable good fortune, the hospice doctor was a close friend and had been a sculpting student of Rachman's and the hospice chaplain was also a close friend to him. We felt great relief knowing that Rachman would have excellent care. And he would have honest reassurance and the best support possible.

In our sacred state or place the feeling was: "Okay none of this matters very much any more...what's important now?"

He was changed by all that had transpired, and he was given a more quiet state to be in at each stage of his leave-taking. He never fought against what was happening... he was in inwardly made ready for his death.

People wanted to come and visit him. I always consulted Rachman about this. There were a few people who had issues with him that they wanted or needed to work out before he died. Two of his friends came to the door one day with long faces. I invited them in but I told them: "Please don't feel sorry for Rachman, cheer up, we're having a good day." However, they couldn't shake their shock at seeing him. Some visitors would bring their own issues, their own fears about death, when they talked to him. After a few visits like this, Rachman said, "I don't want to do this any more. I don't have the energy to help people work out their own issues about death."

A very close friend, Leanna, came to be with us for a week. She had had a falling out with Rachman at one time and it seemed like there was a way for amends to be made for both of them. Rachman sincerely apologized for getting in the way of our friendship and there was heartfelt forgiveness flowing all around.. It was a very special time. During that visit Leanna encouraged me to take Rachman to our church for one last visit. This meant hauling oxygen bottle, wheel chair and supplies for comfort. I couldn't have done it without her help. He was able to take communion, say goodbye to friends and wheel around the outdoor labyrinth. During this wonderful week, we all stayed up and talked about life and many things, ate good meals and played music into the night. Little did we know that Rachman was within a few weeks of leaving this world.

Shortly after Leanna's departure, our children came home to help, to be there for Rachman. At this point we really hoped we had some months ahead with him... Dare we dream a year? There was little outward sorrow. Our family did their best to try to hold it together for him. Away from him there was a lot of talking; there were a lot of tears. We looked to each other for love, comfort, and support, how to be with this. Some of us had thought little about death. We all felt our inadequacies... I asked myself, "How can this be happening? What can I do to make things easier?" It was hard to know what to say, how to communicate the swirling of love and conflicting feelings.

My daughter Helise had early mornings to visit while I dashed for supplies or a little exercise. She managed to face what he was going through and came very close to him. He confided in her. They had many close private conversations. She asked Rachman how he wanted to be thought of after he was gone. He said, "Miss me, but not too much."

Daniel came home filled with an intense fierce determination... He was going to be there for his father, help his dad through what he was going through... give him everything he could. Rachman had seen Daniel through his severe accident just months before. And now Daniel was taking the lead to help his father through his illness.

Our son Gordon was working toward his doctorate in anthropology but dropped all of his responsibilities to come home for his father. And Hamilton had quickly come home setting aside his work and concerns.

Since we hoped that we had some months ahead, and the medical team gave us the most optimistic outlook of possibly 8 months, our children left with a plan to return in a few months. With in a few days of returning to his home in Hawaii, Daniel was grief-stricken and asked himself: "What am I doing here?" He felt he had to return to Texas, to be there with Rachman. I was greatly relieved at his return. I was in a state of total exhaustion. Daniel arrived back with us. He saw what I couldn't see, that Rachman's time was going to be much shorter than we had realized. Daniel called his siblings to come home as soon as they could. Everyone made their arrangements.

The very human attempt to gain control emerges when one perceives they are losing it. Feelings come out sideways as one tries so hard to hold on to dignity, control, preferences...time. Rachman was unaware that he was trying to hold onto what little control he had by giving many little commands. I would finally sit down and he would think of something else. I finally admitted to him that he seemed to be constant with his requests.

I was so tired and just wanted to sit down and be with him. He was immediately sorry and hadn't realized how intense he had gotten..

As the days passed Rachman began to relax more. He was unable to manage without strong medications to relieve reoccurring breathing crisis. Little by little he became free of ego, free of blaming others or himself, became calm and accepting. He still maintained his sense of humor... and rather extraordinarily, he was able to participate with our spiritual team in the Subud organization we belonged to and did so until close to his death.

He loved being of service this way and worked harmoniously with our team.

With all the struggle to breathe, I knew Rachman couldn't possibly go on much longer. There were signs that his organs were slowing down, not functioning effectively. I was in touch with Rachman's hospice doctor. The hospice team was very attentive – I could call them any time. Their assessment was that he was hours away from passing. When someone is "actively dying", the time convention is stated as hours, not days or weeks.

We were as well prepared as we knew how to be.

At one point when there was no longer any relief from the shutting down of his body Rachman asked me, "Is this the way it's going to be?" With as much tenderness as I could muster, I said, "Yes, my love, this is the way it's going to be". He nodded in acknowledgment. At which point he seemed to realize more fully that he was closer to his passing.

THE NIGHT BEFORE RACHMAN DIED...

I made a family dinner for all of us. Rachman wasn't hungry. He had an icecream sandwich. It seemed like he was reducing his actions, words and preferences down to the most essential things from his perspective... He knew his time was at hand.

Rachman asked to have a family movie night and it felt like the emphasis was on the children (even though they were all adult)... He asked that we set up our bedroom to have a movie and dessert. The movie he requested was Transformers... an action packed film were things turn into other things to defend their territory. We all flopped on beds, easy chairs and the floor, dimmed the lights and started the movie. Rachman fell asleep while eating yet another icecream sandwich, chocolate all over his face...When he awoke later he was frightened when he discovered this brown stuff on his face, to which one of the children on noticing said, "It's ok, Dad, it's just chocolate." There was a little quiet amusement. We all assembled to prepare for whatever the remainder of the night would bring.

One of my sons at some time later said, "A perfect epithet for Dad, 'HE DIED

WITH CHOCOLATE ON HIS FACE'."

That evening he awoke from a nap and went into a severe breathing crisis—unable to get enough air. We had special equipment to address this issue, but it was Daniel who had enough calm and presence of mind to figured out how to make it work and settle Rachman down. The doctor was called. I needed to know that there would be a way to keep him as comfortable as possible. The doctor came in the early morning to examine him and adjust his medications and said that it wouldn't be long. The active dying process was unfolding.

He was drifting in and out of sleep.

Knowing that he would be slipping in to unconsciousness, I asked him if he would like to say goodbye to his mother. I called her on the phone so they could say their goodbyes to each other.

His mother did all the talking. At last he said to her, "I'll see you at the pass... I love you mom" and with that Rachman closed his eyes and drifted between this world and the next. Never to speak again.

We'd all been up for 24 hours or more. Our family found places to take a nap... I promised to wake everyone when there was any indication of Rachman getting ready to pass.

My latihan came, and a song flowed out of me. A song that reached up to God asking for Rachman's safe passage, thanking God for our marriage, our children, for all our years together.

I wiped his forehead and dripped a few drops of water into his mouth. Held his hand.

It was late – well after midnight. I asked the nurse to wake me when his breathing changed. "We all want to be there when he passes." I had to close my eyes. Fifteen minutes or so later she tapped me on the shoulder.

"He's getting close." The kids and I gathered round.

Everyone was quiet. We listened and watched. His last breath was witnessed by all of us. He was kissed. The grief, disbelief, exhaustion all ran together. We all burst into tears and sobs.

We asked to keep Rachman until morning. We sat with him until dawn, about 6 hours or so... It was peaceful. I don't remember if we talked or not.

Three days after Rachman died he was to be cremated as requested. Our children didn't want to attend and I could understand them not wanting to go.

But I was strongly compelled to go knowing that if it had been me, Rachman would have seen it through to the conclusion. Early the morning of his cremation, I readied myself to go to the crematorium and to my surprise all of my children got into the car with me. My sister and brother-in-law arrived as well.

We walked into the room and the person in charge said: "You can see him on the table now," and lifted the curtain for viewing.

The kids were mildly relieved to see him. He looked as though the illness had left his body and he looked like the Rachman we all remembered. They seemed very glad they'd come.

Then I went deep into "our" state. I was very connected to him. The kids left the room. I experienced energy coming through my feet and rising through me, moving out to Rachman then back to me. I felt like a tree, and the energy was moving up through my roots up into my branches, cycling back and forth between us. I felt him saying, "I'm okay, this is real, it's powerful, this is what it's like on the other side." A voice said, "Just let it go on." I felt I was moved by my inner to experience this. I had no sense of grief or loss. I felt the energy of life, of grace, the essence of what is most important. There was a sense of life, larger and more vibrant beyond our life on earth. This was probably the most powerful experience I've ever had. Slowly the feeling let up.

My sister was still there, as though standing guard over me, at least it felt that way, helping me. I was grateful she stayed with me.

Then they rolled him over to the big chamber and I watched the door close, and I decided it was right to leave.

Everyone was standing out in the parking lot. There was a lightness of feeling. We went out to a restaurant to have Rachman's favorite breakfast and then for a walk in the park.

It was strange how the feelings lifted, at least for a while, after Rachman died. I had a lot of material decisions to make, and I discovered he was still there. I'd ask: "What do you think I should do about this" and he would answer. I noticed that Rachman was free of his ego and was much "lighter" and very enthusiastic. A friend told me Rachman visited him after his death. He was asked to help me… In another dream by a close friend, Rachman was in a white tuxedo suit and he came up to my friend on a skateboard and asked him to help me. Lots of friends had dreams or experiences in which Rachman came to them saying: "Don't be afraid. We are all one." The very clear sense was that Rachman was quite busy and quite engaged in his next life…yet he remained available to me as I needed him.

Months later Rachman gave his approval of Benedict becoming my new husband. He was no longer possessive and encouraged me to move forward with enthusiasm.

Last Ramadan I saw Rachman in the distance…
we rushed towards each other
we came close to each other
we saw we were both okay
we were both greatly relieved.
we wanted to hug one another but we couldn't because we realized we were in different worlds. There was an exchange of very strong loving feelings. That was the last contact we had.
May He be blessed.

DANIEL

Mom

Reading your remembrances, I felt I could share a bit more with you about some of what I experienced, although what you wrote doesn't need to be revised to reflect any of this. I knew that dad was dying and that he was short for the world from the very start. The reason I was so grief-stricken the first time that I returned home was because I had known this, and I couldn't believe that I had left knowing this. I was overcome with a feeling of guilt and grief, and I knew I HAD to return immediately. I never had any illusion that he might get more time. I had made my peace with this early on. This is what made it possible for me to play the role that I did.

The reason I knew so clearly was partly because of the state that I was in as a result of my own accident and struggle, and partly because of a prescient moment that I had had with dad one night back when he was staying with me in my hospital room at Queens. He had had that cough and I remember feeling deep concern for him as I lay there in my bed listening to him cough, and a bit of exasperation that the doctors weren't concerned for him (as I was). Much later when I heard of his diagnosis I knew that he was dying, and that it would be soon.

Years earlier I remember pondering and thinking that I would likely one day be sitting next to him as he died of lung cancer. A morbid thing to be thinking I know, but I felt strongly that it was a likelihood. All of these things kind of clicked into place for me when dad was diagnosed in Bakersfield. I knew where things were heading, and I knew I had a role to play in some way. I felt that my participation in dad's death somehow brought things full circle. I feel clean and without any "unfinished business" with dad. It's kind of odd. We shook hands in a forearm to forearm grasp a few days before he passed as I was there with him administering a dose of his drugs, and he thanked me for being there with him. I felt a deep brotherhood with him in that moment.

I also had two very real and incomprehensible experiences with dad during that time that I've shared with you before (most recently at your wedding). One, that early morning when I had to leave back to Hawaii the first time (in September), and another when he was only hours from passing. I call them incomprehensible because I experienced them in a deep place and in a way that my mind cannot understand, and I strongly want to avoid creating a narrative to try and explain them or make sense of them. Having experienced them is enough. Anyhow, I wanted to share these thoughts and memories that reading your account stirred up in me.

Love,
Dan

HELISE

When Harry died, I was at work. I got the phone call from my mother. It was my tipping point. I broke down sobbing at work as I just couldn't believe all that was happening. We had faced too much as a family with Daniel's motorcycle accident, my grandfather passing, and then my Dad's diagnosis. I remember feeling like that was it for me. The news just sent me into a state I didn't expect. I was never close to Harry — but I loved my father, and I knew this would hurt him very deeply. He adored his dad. I could hear the desperation in my mother's voice when she called to tell me Harry passed. I knew immediately that I needed to get to her and help her figure out what to do to get my Dad the care he needed… and just help her. I flew out to Bakersfield within a few days to help. When I arrived, my mother was worn out. The emotional fatigue of all these life events was dragging her down. She had no energy to fight through the mess of getting my father a portable oxygen device that he would desperately need to get back to Texas. I had to figure out how to get him home and get him the portable device he would need for the trip. He couldn't fly, so I knew we would be driving from Bakersfield to Texas. Through the financial help of SUBUD friends, along with my tenacity fighting through some issues with my father not having medical insurance, I was able to secure him a device that would work. It took many phone calls, and some navigation — persistence… but we did it. Gordon and I were going to drive my parents home so that my dad could get the medical care he needed at home. There was no point in him staying at his parent's home. His father had passed. His mother was frail. His sisters would be coming and going… and my mother needed to be at her own home for this "adventure" she was about to embark on. Gordon and I quietly made an agreement. We were driving straight through the desert. Not stopping but to eat or use the restroom… we'd trade off turns driving, but we had to get Dad home fast. We felt as though my mom should not drive because she had been through way too much to focus on safety. We knew Dad was medicated and in no state to make decisions about driving safety. We took control. Good or bad, it was what we felt needed to happen. We were concerned that if we had any sort of medical emergency or episode in the desert that we would be too far aware for medical help… or out of cell phone range to call for help. It was nerve-wracking. Within 23 hours we drove from Bakersfield, California to San Antonio, Texas. It actually was a "fun" trip in that Gordon and I worked very well together as a team. We took control of the trip and left little option to our parents on how we intended to get them home so fast. I think that was partly in an emotional effort to try to "save them" from the situation… We just wanted to help… and try to bring some comfort to my mother who had been holding things together since my father's diagnosis in California — and caring for her son who nearly died — and saying goodbye to her father who passed — and now this.

In between traveling to California, securing the breathing machine, and traveling back to Texas I was able to coordinate some local benefits for medical care. I was also able to set up an appointment at a Cancer Treatment facility with a top local doctor through a business executive I knew. This individual did community affairs work for the organization I work for and helped get my dad seen quickly at the cancer center. The coordination was an opportunity for me to utilize my strengths of organizing, planning, and leading through stressful situations with competing demands.

Nevertheless, Dad was home, and was going to get the chemo he needed. I became full of anxiety. It was very difficult to work. I felt like I needed to be very present for my parents… and spend time with them. I offered to go to appointments with them. Organize information. Make phones calls. Whatever was needed. I knew my father was going to die. I knew the chemo would not work… but I was hopeful for any quality he could gain by prolonging his life. But realistically I knew that we had to make him comfortable, and prepare for the worst. I decided to take a leave of absence from work. I wanted to be available for my mom — and spend time with my dad. There were times where my mother would go run errands in the morning and I would stay and sit with my dad… making sure he had whatever he needed. There were times were we sat in silence. He would be surfing on his iPad that we got him (as a distraction), or sleeping peacefully. I waited for the right time to tell my parents that they needed wills, power of attorneys, and medical directives. It would make things easier in the end if needed. I didn't want my mom to struggle through any challenges later. My dad was very open to the conversation and willing to let me help them set up legal documents online. At the same time, I began going to counseling with a counselor my brother once saw. Dr. Zitlin was a straight shooter who I liked a lot. He was helping me deal with the stress of caring for a terminally ill parent, while preparing me on how to say goodbye… how to act… how to process all that was going on. The best thing Doctor Zitlin did for me was TELL ME to tell my father how much I loved him, that I wished I had been a better daughter, and that I was going to miss him. Dr. Z told me then, and I know it know, that conversation would be invaluable to me…and it was. I recall the story my mother mentioned about going to my parent's church one last time. It was pure torture… Sitting in the pews. People looking at my dad. Praying over him. Talking with him. I had a lump in my throat the entire time, trying not to cry. After church we ate breakfast in the church hall. Bacon!! Dad's favorite. My mom was off talking with people and my dad asked me "Honey are you ok? Are you sad"… He knew I was having a very hard time that day. He was still concerned about me. It was really difficult to hold it together and try not to just lose it... looking back, maybe I needed to lose it... cry it out... but I just sucked it up and continued to try to support my parents. I made arrangements and prepaid for his cremation. In the end, I didn't want my mom to have to deal with any of those details. When we knew his time was even shorter than expected I made the arrangements. It was one of the worst days of my life. I never told my dad that we did that. He didn't need to know. I remember leaving the funeral home feeling so guilty. It was pouring down rain. I called Gordon, sobbing. It was the worst experience in the world making those arrangements. It made me sick.

I recall one day sitting at my parent's home with my mom, Leanna, and my dad. We were listening to a Hawaiian version of "Somewhere over the Rainbow". Dad sat at the computer with his feet up. He had a prayer blanket that friends at the church made for him draped over his legs. He had his eyes closed with a smile on his face listening to the song. My mom and I looked at each other with tears in our eyes... the words were so powerful at that moment in the song. We knew it would mean something later to us... and it did, when we played it at his memorial.

When my father passed, we were all around him. I didn't know how I would respond. I was scared. He took his last breath... And then all I heard was my youngest brother sob. My mother wailing. My brother's crying. While we all were so happy that my father was released from the suffering of the cancer, it was a moment in time that will forever be burned on my heart. Daniel kissed my father's forehead and thanked him for caring for him through the trauma of his motorcycle accident. I touched my dad's hand, too scared to do anything else. After we sat with his body for several hours, the funeral home came to collect his body. It was very difficult to allow that to happen. I kept thinking "What if he wakes up and needs us"... it was hard to let go. I was so worried about my mother... and how she would get through this. I went home after not having had much sleep that night... I had to tell my son the news, shower and then get back to my mother and brothers. When I got home my husband hugged me. My son walked up to me and asked how grandpa was doing. My husband and I both hugged my son at the same time and told him that Grandpa had passed away last night. We all cried together, hugging, and just standing there comforting my son.

I have never felt so much pain in my life as I did the morning after my dad's passing. I could not understand how the world was still spinning and he was not in it anymore. I woke up crying... as death stared me in face. There was no escaping the reality of it all. My husband was still asleep, so I thought, but he reached over and grabbed my hand. It was very, very difficult for the first 5 days after Dad died. It was so final — and so unfair. As my mother wrote, things began to change after my dad was cremated... my head began to comprehend the magnitude of his passing. Letting go became more natural and less forced...

I miss my dad. I look at his picture everyday. I hear his voice. I miss him when I need his clever mind to solve a technical issue or help fix something at my house. I laugh at how challenging his personality was — and how much I am like him in many ways. Never in my life have I ever experienced someone with so much strength and bravery face death. He was incredible — fearless... and I feel blessed to have been able to have him as my father.

LEANNA HARRISON

I'm watching it... a bohemian-looking man begins falling in love with my then and always best friend, Aminah, as we hike together through the redwood forest in Northern California. They are smitten and soon after, they begin their life together. Over three decades of raising families, midnight Ramadans, and squirming to each find our "right work", I again find myself sitting with them still watching the sparks fly.

I got the call — it isn't pneumonia — it's more serious — and I want to be there. Expecting sadness and confusion, I enter their home full of color: wall murals, mosaic, rock sculptures by Rachman, and paintings by Aminah. Immediately I am transported into a womb-like environment of warmth and acceptance with only the essential things being said and done. We are being carried together on the wings of an angel and it is extraordinary. The three of us begin staying up very late in the evenings sharing the treasured memories of raising our young children together, what Latihan really means, the richness of our lives, and lamenting how quickly time passes. Rachman begins sharing essential bits of wisdom, the in and out of his oxygen machine accenting his strong words. There is also humor, lightness, viewing celestial patterns, and watching "Django Unchained" together on his iPad. Seeing him perched on the edge of the sofa, round-headed, sharing his wisdom each day, he earns the title from me of Baby Buddha. He wears it well. He often interrupts these sessions to continue his important Subud work on phone and online as a National Helper even until his last few weeks on this Earth. Rachman, the man in control, keeps detailed charts of his medications and when to take each one. A life insurance flyer arrives in the mail. He looks at Aminah and jokingly asks, "Do you think it's too late?" I arrive after both Aminah and Rachman have fully accepted what is happening to them. Aminah's undemanding love and dedication to his comfort and menu requests is impressive. He is thrilled he can eat the things normally not chosen for health reasons; fried chicken, chocolate sauce on his ice cream, and a request for red wine. One morning he gets up, goes straight to the computer, and begins listening to all his favorite songs over these many years. What could we do? Helise, her daughter, Jada, Aminah, and I begin dancing in celebration while I suppress tears knowing it is the last time he will ever hear each song.

I've been frightened of the death experience for most of my lifetime, but Rachman taught me to be bold and to appreciate the days and hours we are given. Aminah taught me to be gentle, loyal, and strong in respect and dedication to those we love. So what could I offer as a fitting tribute to Rachman at his passing but a star forever in our celestial heavens named "William Michael Rachman Ulmer, a sculptor and artist".

Life in Death

There are bound to be some among you who will be wondering, 'Can we feel anything when we are dead, given that when we die everything stops? Our mouth cannot speak any more, let alone taste anything. Our nose can no longer smell, because our breathing has stopped. Our eyes too can no longer see, and the same applies to our ears and the rest.'

If you look at it just from the physical point of view, it is true. A dead person can do nothing other than lie on a mattress or on the floor. But you need to reflect deeper. Your hand is alive through its feeling; thus if the feeling is gone, your hand is no longer alive. So a dead person's hand can no longer move and their mouth can no longer speak because their feeling has left: the feeling in their mouth has gone, the feeling in their hand has gone. This is what we need to understand. Where has it gone? This is the purpose of the latihan. In the latihan you are trained to be normal, so that during your life in this world you can feel where the feeling of life is in your hand, where the feeling of life is in your mouth.

It has been said, by people who were given God's grace and it is also written in the holy books, in the Psalms, the Torah, the Gospels and the Quran, that in our life in death – by which Bapak means our life after death – we can continue to feel.

> Bapak
> Los Angeles, CA U.S.A.
> June 6, 1967

SADNESS

UNEXPECTED WINTER

~ MIRANDA HAMPTON

I plunged my hand deep down
into an empty barren land.
The blind snapped open
the world awoke as I
snatched a shadow by its tail

the blind became a veil
winter whiter than white
moving as if someone
had disturbed its stillness
as they moved through and on

I was not afraid
knowing you were near —
then the dawning
and the tears as I awoke
knowing you had gone.

Next day someone both dark and bright
rang to say to look outside
at the winter whiter than white —
then he said as if he knew my dream
that I would go outside

and jump and shout
as if I were a child
returning back inside
all wet and cold, would cry
       knowing you had gone.

GRIEF

~ ILONA MERLIN

I'm so sad when I am happy
because I'm happy without you.
I feel so lonely when beauty surrounds me,
I don't know how to
be happy without you.
It's so strange;
I miss you more when
happiness brings tears to my eyes,
tears not of joy but of longing.
Deep, deep longing.
I'm afraid to meet with happiness,
I do not know
how to face it alone.

I'm shy when with happiness,
I am at ease with sorrow.

NATURE OF DEATH

ON DEATH AND DYING

~ SALAMAH POPE

My impression, my feeling, my conviction even, is that we don't know much. Bapak had a lot to say about it – death, and the Afterlife – but what I heard him say was different every time. So my guess is that, just as we are all different, and our life differs from everyone else's, so too will our Afterlife be different from everyone else's. In other words, there's no use thinking about it!

Having said that, it is – for some at least – a fascinating topic, especially for us oldies whose lives are closing down. When I was young I never thought I'd live to be 80; I used to wonder if I'd ever reach that extraordinary thing – the change of millennium. But, here I am, fourteen years after it… and still going strong, still busy. Weird.

There's a huge literature out there, too – on death and dying, and the Afterlife. Abdullah liked books by Raymond Moody, Elizabeth Kubler-Ross and particularly Kenneth Ring and Michael Newton. The most convincing book I suppose is "Proof of Heaven" by a neuro-surgeon, Eban Alexander: and there was an amazing TED lecture by another neurologist who had had a stroke, and watched herself going through it all. What she learned from this was that heaven could be experienced by the right side of our brain: i.e. when our ordinary, left-brain thinking is stopped. (But, again, *their* experience of the Afterlife might not be yours or mine.) And, if you put "books on death and dying" into Google there are, literally, hundreds. But, So What?

The purpose of them all seems to be to show us, convince us that there IS an Afterlife. But this, in Subud, we know. If we haven't actually had experiences of other lives and other deaths, we have at least heard and/or read Bapak's talks. And he took it absolutely for granted.

As do I. I **know** there is a hell (because I've been there), and I **know** there is a heaven, because I've been there, too, a few times. But it changes, every time! So, again, there seems little point in thinking about death and dying.

What *is* valuable, of course, is the knowledge, the understanding, the conviction that there *is* an Afterlife ahead of us all, which will be in accord with – and entirely depend upon – the life we have lived here in this world. And thus encourage and inspire us to live our life here and now, better. More ethically. More compassionately. More consciously. More worshipfully even! Remembering, as often as we can, the presence of God. And **asking forgiveness, constantly** – for our forgetting.

When he was younger, living in the early days of the Wisma Subud, Bapak sometimes gave unrecorded talks to the helpers. Men helpers one Sunday a month, and women helpers another Sunday a month. He talked about his youth, and he talked about his spiritual experiences and, sitting relaxed and comfortable with Ibu ("my" Ibu, Ibu Siti Sumari) beside him, he chatted and talked, about oh almost anything.

Once I remember he talked about hell, and how real it was. But not too different from this life, he added. "For instance, if you like watching the boxing on television in this life, or going to the cinema – and little else – then, when you die you just go on doing that. Unchanging. Stuck. So not too unpleasant!" But another time he warned us women about the spiritual dangers of sex. "For women who have had sex with many men", he said, "when they die the *jiwas* of those men come to her, and tear her apart – because they each have a claim to her."

And the opposite, of course. I can't now remember the details which Abdullah passed on to me of what Bapak said about the grim fate awaiting men who had had many women in this life: but he certainly did. Unless they had been diligent in the latihan and purified of them, the women.

Sometimes, though, he'd talk of heaven. Unfortunately the only story I can remember now about this is when he looked at Ibu Musa, sitting near me on the floor. (Ibu Musa was an American woman living in the Wisma Subud, the widow of an Indonesian diplomat.) "When Ibu Musa leaves this world", he said, "she will have a beautiful house in the next, bigger and nicer than the one she lives in now, because she looks after her little house here so well."

Another time, in fact several times, he referred to the closeness of the next world as being very near to this one. "It's thin, the separation, just like the sheet or transparent white screen of the *wayang purwa* [traditional shadow-puppet dramas]. There is no distance at all between this life and the other life: it is very close." On one side of the screen we see the shadows, grey and semi-transparent; on the other are the magnificent puppets themselves clad in fabulous multi-coloured clothes, gold painted, shining, and glorious.

And this is how one of my experiences of heaven was, too. I was, at the time, ill in bed, hemorrhaging, dying slowly, peacefully – happily even. And yet I was also walking, alone but with a small loose cluster of other people, up a mountain. We were walking along in a shallow river, *which was running up hill,* helping us move forward, up the mountain – the faint peak of which we could see up ahead of us in the distance. And the amazingly beautiful rainforest around us at the edges of the river was bright, vivid greens and with flowers – of unbelievable colours. Colours I have never seen in this world, vivid – and so lush and absolutely alive.

This reminds me of Laura Labby, and when she was ill, very ill, again in the Wisma Subud. She was dying, and happily, too. But Latifah Myerson (as Taormina was then) was not happy about this – and, miraculously, got on the phone to Bapak himself, who was in New Zealand at the time. "Not Laura's time to go," he said briefly. "Get her to hospital." Later, when Laura came home again, better, although still weak, I was sitting by her bedside one morning when Mas Adji (Bapak's grandson) came in. "Good to see you, Laura. Not your time to die," he scolded her. "Bapak explained to me that we each have a right time to die – and this was not your time." Then he went on to say: But we don't always die at the right time. "Rochanawati, my mother, died eleven years too early, and Yangti, my grandmother, died nine years too late." [Note: apologies! I may have got those numbers of years mixed up; they may have been the other way around.] "So we don't always die at our right time," Adji concluded. "But Bapak said it is better for us [i.e. in the Afterlife] if we do."

Another story. One day, sitting on the porch of our apartment in the Wisma Subud, Bapak remarked that, if Abdullah had died then, he would be able to hear me – but not see me. And then he looked at me and said, "If Salamah died now, she would be able to see you, Abdullah, but not hear you." Then he asked me, "Do you see things, Salamah? Have you seen Bapak's guardian animals?" But, alas, I hadn't. "*Masih takut*" (still afraid) Bapak said briefly, going back to the drawings of the latihan hall which they'd been looking at.

Later, curious about this seeing business, I asked Pak Sudarto, one of the most experienced helpers: Why, and what does this mean? "Well," he explained, "this means that Abdullah's ears have been purified by the latihan, but not yet his eyes. And your eyes are purified, but not yet your ears." Being thick, I still didn't understand. Patiently he explained: "You can *see* things, Salamah, that are not there. Like people's faces, you know what is inside them. But," he chuckled, "you are still afraid of seeing things that are not here, not in this world!"

Another story, briefly. I remember walking down by the great latihan hall early one morning and meeting Patricia Lacey, who was visiting – and had been in a bit of a sad state when she arrived. But now she was aglow. "Oh Salamah", she said, "I saw Bapak yesterday, and he told me that we would all be together, all meeting up again, after we'd left this world. Isn't that amazingly wonderful!!"

Many years ago I experienced something like this myself – but that story is written up in Emmanuel's other wonderful collection, *An Extraordinary Man*, so I won't tell it again here.

I think, and I feel, and I trust, and I hope: that we will *go to Bapak*, when we die. I remember Sudarto telling us an experience of his, to this effect. And another time Varindra telling us the same thing – but with a little extra twist. "Bapak said we would all go to him when we died, that he would lift us up by our hair. 'But what about you, Varindra?' he joked, 'You have no hair!'" Varindra was a notorious womanizer, but I think he had taken the hint.

So the quality of our Afterlife does seem to depend on how we have lived our life in this world. For instance, I had a friend married to a rather nasty man, and she asked Bapak if she could divorce him. Bapak told her that he would not advise her about this; the decision was hers. But that, if she looked after her husband as she would a child, a son, as a brother, she would earn her *jodoh* (soul-mate) in the next life.

I like that idea – of earning a good Afterlife. And it is, after all, simply what the great religions have been telling us for millennia.

And a final little story, about Bapak testing us, occasionally, over the years: How would it be for us if we died *now*? And what we experienced then changed, of course, as we grew older – older in years, and older in our practice of surrender in the latihan, in our purification, and in our progress in the spirit.

So there is a heaven, and there is a hell: and I know that all we think and all we do – and not do – is known, and registered. Recorded. So it behooves us, I am certain, to remember this, and to do *prihatin*. To fast and to pray. And to guard our thoughts, our feelings, our behaviour and above all our Subud latihan, our worship of Almighty God. Earning a good place in the Afterlife.

July 6, 2014

WHAT IT IS ALL ABOUT

~ DAPHNE TIBBS

Now you have seen the other side,
Do you know what it is all about?

Hundreds of times
— endless, uncountable times —
all of them carrying the weight of
unfinished voyages
and seemingly irreversible decisions,
we (they, us)
have crossed this bridge without hope.

Wave to me from across the water,
Blow me a kiss.

Ah, but we know better, my love,
we know better.
The truth moves in our breath,
the colors of the rainbow are always there
dispersed in the eternal light.

I place crystal prisms
and star encrusted pyramids
where the light can find them
and I run my fingers through the rainbows.
I hope, I hope, I hope
for my children and my children's children
and yours too:
that they may reach into their hearts
(or pockets)
and find their rainbows there.

AWAKENING

~ NURAINI MAGNUSSON

Death awakens
in us,
the will to live

Death speaks
in a tongue
that we cannot always hear,
that we do not always
want to hear.

Death belongs
not in this time,
but in all time,
As the butterfly,
with radiant colour of wing,
in prelude
to its next life,
so the communion of souls
in life's Hereafter,
come together,
in joyous song
and union,
and gift of humility.

Each soul
has its own time,
and its own season,
and speaks
its own rhyme,
in its own
ultimate expression
of love,
for our Divine Creator,
the Creator of all.

In our departing…
                        each soul
              has its own awakening…

GATES OF WINTER

~ THERESA WHITEHILL

The two gates of winter are guarded by the dead.
All Hallows' Eve in early November
and Memorial Day when summer is allowed to leak itself
out into free air. Death by love, by life, by reason
on the one side; death by patriotism, by ideals, by
economy on the other.

We stand and feed the dead in order to fend off winter
and to banish it, to free ourselves of ornamental
limits. We feed the dead our memories and our
sorrows, with barbeques and sweets, with a holiday
dedicated to softening bones over a fire, chocolates
wrapped in iridescent foil. But what is it the dead
actually savor, what's delectable once you've
divided yourself in two and no longer have to stand
on the hill imagining wisdom?

I have been listening to the dead and find them difficult.
They are not as articulate as they could be.
What is it that sets their skin aflame,
that causes them to flutter their eyelids half open
with helpless desire? I would think it would be flowers,
and babies, and the more expensive kind of soap bubbles,
red objects, fireworks, swooning, those things inescapably fertile
and passing. We are this planet's goodbye and its trident.
We know how to feed things, spirits and loneliness, structural steel
and alphabets, now we must learn somehow to be fed.

WHAT HAPPENED TO ME ONCE

~ MARDIYAH TARANTINO

I'm up here

all alone

suspended in space
There's no blue Heaven that I can see.
Grayish mist everywhere
Way below me: The earth.

Woops! There go my pills down through the ether
Goodbye daily pills that never leave my side!
Oh, oh! There go my cosmetics:
the brush, the liner
I watch them float away, thinking
I'm going to look like hell, now, without lipstick.

"Yoo-hoo! Down there!"
(They don't hear me.)
My kids — I imagine them —
Busy little bugs on a tennis ball.
"I'm stuck!" I yell with no sound:
"You're supposed to pray for me, you know,
Come on now, do the prayers, the Dzikir!
You remember how, we've done them together,
For the third day, and for the seventh day...
Get me going!"

But I've no body, No Body at all!
To tell the truth, it's scary, suspended here.
Scary, but kind of free.

Hello, here's my Latihan! Here we are now,
We're One. That's all that's left.
An Awareness.
Wow! Can we do it alone like this?
Just the two of us?

Ah well, they're disappearing now
Covered with mist
It's lonely up here, waiting.
Bismillah, La Illaha Ilallah.

The Jiwa's Own Life

Eventually, when you die, the jiwa will have its own way. It will live its own life. Because, at that moment this physical body ~ the nafsu and the heart and mind ~ don't work any more.

The end of our life is like a car when it has no more petrol, the petrol pump is turned off, so that even if your body is still complete, is still perfect, it will stop working because the nafsu is done. Even more if the car is beginning to fall apart, as if its build-in obsolescence has arrived. Okay, it falls apart and that is even more clear. But the point is, the moment of death is when the nafsu stops working.

Then you rely on your jiwa. What will continue to live is your jiwa.

So, it is essential that this jiwa should know and understand your life in this world. So that you go ahead complete; aware of what you have been, where you have been, who you have been, what you have done. And this can only happen if in this life your jiwa accompanies everything you do.

Your jiwa needs to get to know who you are, what you are doing, what you know, what you see, what you do. So that when you come to the end of your life you are complete and you take forward with you in the jiwa a perfect memory of everything that you have experienced in this world.

Bapak
Woodstock, VT U.S.A.
June 25, 1981

ANGELS

OTHER LIVES

~ ANONYMOUS

One Sunday in 2006, I was doing latihan at the Muhammad Subuh Centre, Kalimantan, and during the latihan, was suddenly taken over to the summit of Gunung Merapi, the most holy of volcanoes located just outside Yoygakarta in Java. There were thousands of angels up there at the summit, as far and wide as my eyes could see, and I was told that they were there as there was going to be a natural disaster and many people would die. I was also told that each of the angels was assigned to a person and it had already been determined who would live and who would die, so even if two people were sitting right next to each other, one may live and the other die. I was taken there to be a witness but I didn't know after the latihan, whether it was real or not.

A few days later, a big earthquake hit Bantul in Yogyakarta and 5,500 people died. A part of me was sad, but another part felt very quiet, as I had witnessed that this was already planned and the angels had already gathered beforehand to oversee it. A few more days passed after the quake, and as I was doing latihan, I was instructed very clearly: "Pray for your descendants who died in that earthquake", I did as I was told, but then after the latihan finished, I realised what I had been told didn't make "sense" in the normal way. My descendants are my children, and they were alive and living with me in Kalimantan. I didn't have any descendants in Java...

Then an inner reminder came to me of a spontaneous latihan experience I had twenty years earlier of some of my past lives, and how in one of those lives (around 1,000 AD) I was living there in that same area of Central Java as a man in a position of privilege and wealth who had several wives and many children. Then what I was told about praying for my descendants started to make sense. (Descendants from a previous lifetime). For the first time, I suddenly realized that if I have lived other lives in different parts of the world, then people that I meet today anywhere in the world, whether friends, or total strangers, could be my living descendants. I suddenly understood how someone from the other side of the world could be a blood relation not only from this biological present body, but from many previous bodies I may have inhabited over millennia. And it was that awareness I was shown in the latihan that made me realize how much more connected we are than we know.

From *Reminders of Reality*

THE TRAGEDY OF 11 SEPTEMBER 2001

~ LEONARD LASALLE

At around 4 PM on 11 September 2001, I was painting in my studio, fully absorbed by a bouquet of flowers and Frederic Chopin's piano concerto which was playing on a classical music radio program. Suddenly the music was interrupted, followed by an announcement:

"We have just heard from our correspondent in New York that one of the Twin Towers has been hit by a jumbo jet!"

Stunned by the announcement, I switched on the television I normally keep behind a curtain in my studio. What I saw was incredible. The same commercial tower that I had visited some years previously was on fire. The camera that was filming the horrific scene must have been some distance away. The sky was perfectly blue, except for the dense smoke rising from three quarters up the building.

I could not believe my eyes when suddenly another aeroplane hit the second tower in a huge explosion of fire and black smoke. The camera zoomed in on the scene; I was now seeing, amongst the debris falling from the impact, some human forms the size of ants, floating as in slow motion down alongside the colossal building.

My heartbeat suddenly increased, pressurising the blood around my body; I was feeling suddenly terribly angry about man's stupidity and criminal behaviour. Had the world gone totally mad? My whole body was shaking due to my greatly disturbed emotions. It was hard to believe that what I was seeing was actually real and happening. Fully aware of how upset I was, I asked my inner self: "Leonard, what is the best state and place to be in during such dramatic moment?"

Right away I switched off the television stood up, completely letting go of my upset and indignant feelings, ego suffering, and myself altogether. Immediately I felt a neutral deep quietness inside as my consciousness broadened, while my voice went into powerful melodic sounds. The latihan I was doing was very strong and I was fully conscious. My inner eyes opened while the singing went on and I saw a most amazing scene:

From across the Hudson River I could see the city of New York lit by the golden light of the early morning sun. The wind coming from the north-west was pushing the enormous grey black cloud of dust rising from the collapsed towers towards the light of the sun. I saw, in the dusty cloud, the agony of a suffering humanity, yelling and crying out in its profound despair.

Then, I heard harmonious angelic singing. I looked up to the heavens and saw that they were full of angelic beings coming down with the arms forward towards dramatic scene; their light bodies made golden by the rays of the sun. Although the dark cloud of agony that stretched out from the city carried many faces expressing great confusion and suffering, I could also see, reaching out of the top part of the cloud, upper parts of bodies, arms and hands offering themselves up towards the coming of the assisting angels.

There was a balance between the beauty and the agony. It seemed that the chaos down below was man's creation, the suffering was in the dust and smoke. Souls were being saved by the multitude of angels. They seemed to be there to give assistance and reassurance to the undecided souls that were reaching out of the darkness of the smoke. There was no judgement in the action. Love and care were there to assist the souls who had abandoned their anger and suffering.

I did not switch the television on again. I felt the need to share the understanding that I had gained from this experience; I rapidly took my large sketchbook and started to draw. After a few rapid sketches, I knew that the painting was already waiting in my inner feelings. I took a large white canvas and started to paint. I felt neutral as I watched what I had witnessed reappear on the white linen cloth.

Jesus and the Angel Doctor

There was another really astonishing piece of news, about a member who was ill, and finally he died, and his death was confirmed by a doctor. The man was indeed genuinely dead. This was in Spain, if Bapak is not mistaken. And after he had been taken to the mortuary he came back to life. As he told the story, he did not know or feel that he had died, he felt alive. Then Christ came to him, and then came another, accompanying Christ, an angel perhaps. Then the angel assumed the form of a doctor, an angel doctor. So there was an angel who became a doctor. There are angel doctors. Then this angel cut open the man's chest, perhaps because he had a heart disease. So it may be said that he had had a heart attack from which he eventually died, and was then taken to the mortuary.

His body was about to be washed, but then he was visited by Christ and the angel doctor. After he had been cut open, the contents of his stomach or his chest were taken out and cleaned, with replacements being provided for some of the parts, after which they were put back. The man was then told, 'Don't be afraid and don't worry. You're definitely still alive. God has forgiven you and God is helping you.' That said, Jesus, followed by the angel doctor, then left.

The man did not immediately realize that he had been taken to the mortuary. Then suddenly he got up, saw the attendant, and called to him. On being called by a 'corpse', the attendant, instead of coming, ran away. He ran, well it was night time!

Just suppose Nak Darto had been the attendant, what then Darto? The attendant took one look and on being called he ran off rather than go near. After the attendant had run off, the man had to ask himself,

'Well I never! He's called and he runs away, why's that?'

The man did not feel he had died. Then he was getting down or going to get down from the slab prepared for the dead, but felt 'How can I get down when I'm naked! People will laugh at me.' That would not do, so he lay down again, but, being naked, he thought 'Oh dear, if I'm like this very long I'll catch cold. It's a very funny thing. I'm already cured of the real disease, then I catch cold!'

But the man who had run away had run to look for a doctor. As soon as he found one, he blurted out to him, 'Sir, there's a dead man who's come back to life again.' 'Oh, nonsense! Look, what's this nonsense about?' 'Well, why call it nonsense, since I've come running here about it!'

Then he went back with the doctor, and on arriving the doctor asked, 'Where is he?' 'Over there.' They went up to him and uncovered him, wow! The doctor also ran off. It was comical.

But in the end he was taken out of the mortuary and was then asked how was he able to come back to life. He told them all about it. 'Very strange.' 'Well, maybe I wasn't dead, doctor?' 'Oh, you were dead, you'd been dead for some hours. How could a doctor not know if someone is dead?' 'Well, why am I still alive?' 'That I don't know.' Then he was told to dress, and was taken back home.

Bapak
Cilandak, Indonesia
November 24, 1973
73 CDK

MESSAGES
FROM BEYOND

RAINDROPS ARE FALLING ON MY HEAD

~ ANONYMOUS

The first time I saw the spirit of a dead person, I wondered if I was looking at an angel. But angels look lighter than souls who have passed over, and as I relaxed I could see that it was my friend's Uncle Bill, who had recently died of cancer. I had only met him twice, but we share the same birthday and I had felt a connection with him.

Communicating with someone who has passed over was a new experience for me, and, telepathically, he asked me to buy his wife some flowers that day. I wondered if it was the anniversary of his death or of their daughter's, who had died the same year. At first, I said no to his request. After all, I barely knew the woman and to arrive at her doorstep with flowers just seemed too weird. But then my spirit took over and I said yes. I asked him how she would know they were from him, and he started singing 'Raindrops are falling on my head.' Then he was gone.

I phoned my friend and asked if it was his aunt's birthday or perhaps an anniversary. He said he wasn't sure, so I asked him to phone her. He called me back and told me that it was indeed her birthday and that the song was the one Uncle Bill would sing while putting the children to sleep or doing odd jobs around the house. She cried and said that it was her best birthday present ever.

From *Reminders of Reality*

A VISIT FROM VARINDRA

~ ANONYMOUS

Shortly after Varindra Vittachi's wife died, he came for a visit. There was an intimate group after latihan and Varindra was transformed by his grief. He looked transparent, really sensitive, humble and very sweet. I was sitting across from him as he was sharing some of his wonderful stories. I felt very close to him, felt a lot of love for him and he reminded me of my own father and the whole feeling was of something special being communicated to me specifically. Like a secret being shared, a baton being passed from hand to hand.

He talked about how he prepared himself to tell his stories, how he made himself empty and "waited for Bapak." All the while I felt that connection. I knew him a little socially but not well. At that time in my life, there was nothing to explain why I was being given that particular gift.

A few years later, having had hardly any contact with Varindra, a friend called to tell me Varindra had just passed away. I consoled her as best I could and stepped into the shower. Varindra appeared to me. I said, really now, you could have waited till I'm dressed. Typical! He was serious though and I noticed he was holding a tight little bright red scroll, which he proceeded to push into my chest, just to the left and above my heart. "I can't think of anyone else to entrust with this" is all he said.

My understanding is that we experience things in a "handwriting" that we can read. I'm not claiming I'm the only person to carry on Varindra's legacy, just that this understanding was passed to me.

I would be interested to know if others have had similar or the same experience. All I can do is report what I felt to be a very real experience.

Like Varindra, I do try and empty myself and wait before I write anything, or share any of my work. It has taken all these years of experience, work and the right circumstances to put what I was given into practice. I still had to understand and know for myself first.

From *Reminders of Reality*

MESSAGE FROM ELSIE

~ MANUEL OLIVER

One afternoon, as a freshman in college at UC Santa Cruz, I had a vivid dream while napping in my dorm room. In this dream, I saw a woman I knew to be named "Elsie" in the basement of a large house. She was going to a hidden room to be with a man I understood to be her husband. She told me that all was okay and that the two of them were going to be together again. I don't know how I knew that her name was Elsie, nor had I ever seen her before. Also in this dream, members of my family along with other people I didn't recognize had gathered upstairs sitting in a parlor type room while unaware that there was any activity happening down in the basement below. In this dream, music played, a kind of heavy metal dirge, "God is but Great, God is but love, God is but one."

I woke up sweating, shocked, and feeling an urgency to call my father. My dorm roommate was in our room at the time and he asked me what was wrong, for he saw on my face that I was quite unsettled.

Immediately, I followed my intuition and called my father on the phone telling him about this vivid dream and how I felt that I had to call and tell about it. It turned out that my father had been helping our family friend Richard move a heavy aquarium that day and had found out that Richard's mother, Elsie had just died. Her husband had died years earlier and he used to spend time in a secret room in his basement. Richard, who was a big brother to me in my adolescent years, has had a difficult time letting go of his anger towards his father for dying too soon, for working too hard without taking care to enjoy life or appreciate his loved ones.

I am convinced that Elsie was trying to find someone to deliver the message to her son that all was okay with Richard, and that I, for whatever reason, was the person receptive at the time to hear it. Having this experience, helped open me up to the idea that there was much more reality below the surface than I had suspected or believed.

MY COUSIN'S DEATH

~ ANONYMOUS

My cousin died recently, and I said farewell to her in latihan a couple of weeks ago. She was 32, and had a 13-year-old daughter who has been raised by her parents (the grandparents) for some years now, because my cousin had epilepsy and no job. She was living with a man who also had no job, so they were doing their best to support each other but were really low in every sense of the word. Her life, in other words, was not a success story. One day she went to take a bath alone, suffered an epileptic attack and drowned.

I offered up my latihan for her and knew it was to be our farewell. (I had not been able to attend her funeral.) I started to do the latihan and it was as if she had already been waiting for me. She appeared in a form that showed her without illness, without sorrow, without regret; she was her self that she could have become in this life at its highest level if all had worked out in the best possible way. She was healthy, beautiful, cheerful and the best qualities of her character were realized to the fullest.

A strong sense of nostalgia and remorse for her unhappy fate came upon me, but she kept on raising my head high with her hand and telling me very cheerfully: "Look at the light, not at the shadow, look up, look up, to the light, to the light!" We were communicating without words, and she made me understand, or rather, feel, how wonderfully she is doing and how it can possibly be totally alright and acceptable to even leave a child behind. She also told me that it is wonderful for them – for all family members alive and dead – that I am doing the latihan and that I should keep on doing it. My great-grandparents and grandparents (my grandmother whom I used to talk to a few years after her death, and who also told me then how great it is for them that I am doing the latihan) were also there but only as companion to my cousin; they didn't interfere in any way.

Then we said good-bye. The scene changed for this event, and I saw her standing in a hilly landscape in tall grass and summer flowers; there was a huge tree through which the sun was shining – it was like a Tuscan scene. I could see the grass and the wooden floor of the latihan room meet right in front of my feet. On top of the hill I saw figures standing, waiting for my cousin. We said goodbye and we were all waving our hands, and slowly they were gone. And then the light that I thought was the sun started to come out from behind the tree as if the sun was going down at sunset. But it was not the sun, it was The Light itself, it was God or God's Love as light slowly accessing me, the whole room, everyone else in the room who were doing latihan, and I saw it poured out to the street, all over the world, and it came across my body, everyone else's body, so that we became transparent and full of light. I could also see my sister, her husband, her child and my baby too a few streets further away, for they were babysitting her while I was at latihan: they were all transparent and full of light, and then it came: "You are embodied light."

From *Reminders of Reality*

BEING RABIN

~ ANONYMOUS

I never understood why I received this experience, because I'm not interested in politics and I'm not Jewish. However, it does give me hope to realize that when spiritual progress is made in the Middle East, good can come of it in the next world if not in this one.

I went into a very strong, unusual latihan during a group latihan in November 1995. I was a man, newly dead, hovering above the earth over what seemed to be the Middle East. The location became clearer: a river, which I understood to be the river Jordan, flowed down the middle. Both sides of the river and the surrounding countries (Israel, Palestine, etc) were in a state of twilight darkness. Only one land further to the East, which I understood to be Egypt, was in the sunlight. I felt surrendered and at peace with God.

Many other souls were crowded over the Middle East, persons who had lived on Earth and had died. As I became aware of them, I saw that they were mostly men, Arab Muslims. They were kind of bewildered about where they were and what had happened to them. I was busy working with them, pointing the way, and somehow transporting them onward on their spiritual journey beyond Earth's atmosphere. I was working hard, dedicated to God. It seemed I would be doing this work for a while, and then I would go onward myself.

When the group latihan finished, and I was myself again, I was shaking from the depth and power of my latihan. I asked a helper to test with me what had just happened to me. The helper received a very strong latihan but no specific answers, and I received to be patient, that understanding would be given to me. Then, while driving home from latihan, still deeply affected, the understanding came: during the experience I had been Rabin, the prime minister of Israel who had very recently been assassinated by extremists who opposed his efforts at making peace with the Palestinians. I understood that because he had spiritually developed to the position of peacemaker, he had reached a state where he could both atone for his past (which had caused many deaths) and also help the bewildered souls who had been killed.

From *Reminders of Reality*

I WAS THERE

~ ANONYMOUS

Alone at home on Easter Sunday I had a very strong spontaneous latihan. All of a sudden, Jesus Christ was there before me, in the position of being on the cross. Our foreheads met and I had to raise my arms and hold His hands in mine. Then we parted and I moved to take the wreath off His head and I placed it on mine. I wanted Him to look me in the eye but He did not, and I realized He is dead.

Then the happenings of Christ's sufferings started to happen backwards timewise, but only glimpses: pictures like Him dragging the cross on the street, and a drop of His blood hitting the stone road, and I see it hit the ground in slow motion... I saw the nails go through his body. I had to say out loud: "I was there!" – and when I did, an overwhelmingly strong feeling of pain and grief came over me. I felt His suffering and I wanted to die instead of Him. I was crying hard and I kept saying that I was there.

When the latihan was over, I walked up to the bookshelf and took the Bible in my hands, I have had it since '93, since when I have consulted it maybe five times. A paper fell out of it, I can't remember when and from where I got it and placed it in the Bible. It contained actual messages of Jesus, the main sentence being: "It has come from me." I just opened the Bible, and it opened at Paul's Letter to the Romans 8.

From *Reminders of Reality*

The Symbolism of the Crucifixion

As to the death by crucifixion: this symbolizes that a perfect human being lives, as it were, between this world and the next.

That's why tradition tells us that after he died Jesus was the same as he was before he died.

This shows that it is indeed God's will that the human soul should be able to protect and pass on its individual understanding to all those who are still in coarse form.

Thus Jesus, in his life after death, lost nothing that had become a part of his individuality.

He could still see, hear, smell, speak and perceive; and everything that had been part of him was still there.

Bapak
London, England
August 11, 1959

SPIRITS

LEAVING THE APARTMENT

~ SHOSHANAH MARGOLIN

In 1991, Subud Chicago purchased a house which it later sold. It was a two flat with an apartment on the second floor and an open space intended for a store on the first floor. But it had a ghost!

We bought the house from a man whose wife had recently died. She had loved her second floor apartment and put so much effort into fixing it up and caring for it. She had become and felt her presence. But she did not want to leave.

GRAVEYARD SHIFT

~ ANONYMOUS

The longer I live the more I am convinced that there is this invisible world and that sometimes we are permitted to have a glimpse while we live in the visible world. My maternal grandma used to tell her grandchildren about seeing visions and of course we thought she was coo coo! That is the way children think, but as we grow up often life will show us the truth. After I joined Subud and received the latihan I gradually changed my view with good reason.

Attending the World Congress at Wisma Subud and meeting with other Subud brothers and sisters, for example, certainly left its mark.

An older Subud brother from San Fransisco shared the same hut. One evening, when we had time after dinner, we were shooting the breeze and getting to know each other, and he told me he worked at the SF city mortuary. Gradually, he told about some encounters of a different kind while working there, how he would see people hanging around the building when he worked late and alone. We swapped stories as the evening progressed and I shared a few of my own encounters, although they were nothing like the ones he had experienced much of the time when he was at work. It was commonplace for him to see these ghostly people, both newcomers and older ones. Some of the old ones were chained and walked around like zombies, and he speculated that they came from the Spanish era. What was most amazing was that he took all this in stride and did not show any fear or nervousness about these encounters, while my hair stood up straight just listening to him.

He told Bapak about his strange encounters in the morgue, and Bapak had advised him to be aware of the latihan all the time he worked there, adding that, through his latihan, he may be able to help some of those souls that were hanging around there.

From *Reminders of Reality*

Ghosts and the Material Force

So do not think that the material life forces are very easily disposed of or that they are very easily removed from the inner feeling, from the heart and the thinking. And not only your clothes ~ the bones in your body, too, are material in nature. If later you are able to be aware of it, you will know that many people after death are seen as apparitions of skeletons.

Thus, a man who during his life on earth has not yet received the Grace of God, will later, when he is dead, become a ghost looking like a skeleton. If a woman has become such a ghost, you will, of course, be afraid of her; whereas, when she was still in the flesh and had a skin, she looked beautiful and her smile was enchanting. But when she is dead and has become a mere skeleton, even if she does not smile she is frightening, let alone when she smiles.

This, brothers and sisters, is the material force.

Bapak
Cilandak, Indonesia
August 20, 1967

AT THE GATES

DIALOGUE

~ IILIA THOMPSON

Gatekeeper – You're here. I'm surprised. I was expecting your husband. Why are you here while you are still part of living flesh and blood? It's most unusual, you know, to have someone of your ilk appear.

Illia – I just decided to visit you. To ask you some questions. From the top of the world, your vision might be so great that your knowledge will also be widened and deepened.

Gatekeeper – So, how might I be of service?

Illia – Will my husband enter? And what will be our relationship after he arrives, as I assume he will.

Gatekeeper – Oh yes, your husband will arrive, but he's not due for a while. Still having too much fun down there. He's got his passport, visa stamped by two priests, a rabbi, and a pastor, not to mention that Oriental Subud which seems to bring him peace.

Illia – Yes, he's got the outer intact, but what about mistakes?

Gatekeeper – God forgives, or else my job would be history. The only reason not everybody comes my way is that everyone who makes mistakes must forgive himself and change his ways. A person who repeatedly sins won't be passing through these gates.

Illia – So you have to be busy to allow passage of so many through these gates. What happens next?

Gatekeeper – You sure are nosey! Well, I don't rightly know, but I do know that it is a time of rest. It's very quiet as I peep through the cracks in the gate. There's a gentle light and it is peaceful.

Illia – That's all I need to know. A peaceful restful place. Not a bad place to be. Thank you for your time.

Gatekeeper – It's all that I have. Lots of it. Safe journey.

Illia – Oh, and what about the relationship between my husband and me after he dies?

Gatekeeper – He'll always be a touchstone for you. Always you can speak with him. You've proven that you can travel this far to speak with me. With just a little extra push, you can access him.

Illia – yes. So be it.

ST PETER AT THE GATE

~ THERESA WHITEHILL

He was leaning against the gate
with his hands in his jeans pockets
like he'd been there a long time
or wasn't in a hurry. "All those receipts,"
he said, "that you took such care to
retrieve out of your pockets,
ironing them flat with your hands,
stapling, making notations on them
sometimes… What was that all about?"

NEAR DEATH EXPERIENCES / COMING BACK FROM THE DEAD

MY SECRET

~ ANONYMOUS

A good male friend of ours – not in Subud – had been admitted to hospital with a burst appendix and severe peritonitis had set in. He had been in and out of hospital for a few days with abdominal pains, but because he was very overweight, no one could diagnose that it was appendicitis. He was sent home with pain killers. However, one night he was rushed back into hospital with excruciating abdominal pains and the doctor then decided to operate, saying to his wife that he suspected cancer and she should be prepared for the worst. It was then they discovered that his appendix had burst a day or two earlier. He lapsed into a state of unconsciousness after the operation: a seriously ill man, every organ in his body had failed – his liver, kidneys etc. – and he was kept alive on machines.

After three weeks of being on the machines, the doctor spoke to his wife and family and said that they should consider taking him off the life supports as even if he came out of this, he would be brain dead and would be like a vegetable – there would be no quality of life for him. The family was reluctant to do this.

My husband and I visited him in the Intensive Care Unit of the hospital and saw our good friend lying there, connected to all kinds of machines. I just stood there and felt the latihan, put one finger on his arm and whispered to Almighty God "Show me a miracle God, if it is your will that this man should live, please heal him and give him a second chance at life". I thought no further about it and went home. The family was still considering whether they should take him off the life supports, although many friends pleaded with them not to do this.

The next day I rang the hospital to enquire about his condition. I was told there was a very slight change for the better in his blood count. To cut a long story short, the "dead" man very, very slowly came alive, and after months of rehabilitation was sent back home. He was not brain dead, and the doctors who handled his case were quite baffled and called him their "walking miracle".

He lived for another eleven years! I have never ever let on to him, his family or anyone else, other than my husband, about my whispered prayer, in a state of latihan, which was answered by Almighty God. This is my little secret!

From *Reminders of Reality*

THE LAKE

~ LEONARD HITCHCOCK

It was a hot and sticky [thundery] day and we had just returned from a birthday celebration with Bapak at Wendhausen. There was a large freshwater lake near where we were staying and this was very inviting. I was sitting at one end it seemed not too far to the other side [distances being deceptive] and I decided to swim over. The water was very cold and I made it to about half way across when I realised that I would not have enough energy to make it to the other side [too many late nights probably!]. Unfortunately there was no merit in turning back and there was no one around to alert to my difficulty, being too far from my friends on the bank. Treading water was not an option either as there was little buoyancy in the cold fresh water and I would only be wasting more precious energy. Therefore I had no option but to carry on.

About two thirds of the way across I was really reaching the limits of what I was capable of and have never before or since felt so depleted of energy. At this point I started to leave my body. This was a very real sensation but difficult to describe. Actually it was quite pleasurable but when this started to happen I was 'told' from within, very clearly, that I was not allowed to let it happen and that the way to prevent it was to focus my attention or awareness on the sensation or feel of the water against my skin. This instruction which was very precise was accompanied by a very calm or quiet feeling but I knew it was very important [presumably because it wasn't my destiny to drown at that point!]. Applying this conscious focus onto the sensation of my physical body did indeed stop the occurrence of disassociation and also at that point I seemed to also receive a little more energy. The last part of the distance was an enormous effort and in particular the effort to be present in my body.

I made it, and the experience showed me that we have an understanding and guidance within us which can [and does] look over us and protect us in, sometimes, very practical ways!

I DIED WHEN I WAS 16, BUT HERE I AM

~ RA'UF RAMSEY

By the time I was 16 years old, I had made two serious promises to myself. One was to somehow find a way to improve "how it felt to be me"; in other words, my general level of peace and happiness; and the other was to find out why we are put on this earth. This was because I had experienced inner suffering and unhappiness since I was a small child and really wanted to find some peace and stability.

My father was a Protestant Minister in central Georgia. After choir practice one Saturday night in 1956, I got to go for a joy ride in the 1955 Austin Healy Sports car owned by one of the older young members of the church. We headed out of town on a main highway at 110 + MPH, with the intention of crossing over a small road connecting to another highway and follow it back into town. It had been raining shortly before our excursion, and the asphalt roads were very slippery, because the tar bubbles to the surface in the summer heat and forms a smooth, film that is super slick like ice when wet.

We believed we were near the middle of the hilly road between the two highways, but popped over the last hill before reaching the highway (perpendicular to the road we were on) doing more than 70 MPH. We saw that the vertical dirt bank on the opposite side of the highway about 125 feet away. Maybe we slowed down to 60 MPH before we slammed into the dirt bank.

As we hit the bank, the car bounced back and rolled over, then righted itself again from the force of the collision. I clearly remember the moment of the impact. It felt as though the force of hitting the bank penetrated into the marrow of my bones, and I also remember my head bouncing violently about from hard surface to hard surface inside the car. I passed out, or so I thought, and when I awakened, discovered I had severe injuries to my face (upper lip completely severed from the nose down, most of the flesh was knocked not cut but severed by a blow – from my lower jaw, a tooth knocked out and a whiplash injury and compressed disk in my neck and back). After the driver (who had a broken back, broken wrist and cuts and injuries to his head) and I made it to the hospital and were sewn up, I wondered how we survived, since I understand the brain and other internal organs of the human body cannot sustain an impact and sudden deceleration such as we experienced and still live. I always thought we were just really lucky.

So that was when I was sixteen. Flash forward to age 70. I was at the small construction business where I work. During our lunch break, I had just related this experience to an intern who was working for us, as she had been injured in gymnastics and was talking about bangs to the body.

I went into the bathroom to brush my teeth. As I did so, I began to receive. I was told "You know, you actually did die in that accident, but you were brought back to life. It was like this: (I received something like SWISH, SWISH)." At that moment, I felt sincere remorse that was very deep, since I felt that I had not lived the life that I should after having been brought back to life by God (or an Angel). Then I received (in response to my remorse, I suppose): "The reason you were saved was that you needed to bring your children into this world, and you needed to learn to worship God." So I felt a little better, because I have been practicing and learning to worship God since I was opened at the age of 21, and have fathered 5 children, all of whom also follow the latihan.

SURVIVING A CAR CRASH

~ ANONYMOUS

A friend and I had a shared experience in 1986. We were driving at high speed through the countryside when a tyre blew out. He couldn't control the car which swerved from side to side out of control and in order to avoid a head-on collision with an oncoming semi-trailer, we drove over the embankment into empty space. As we hurtled through the air, we were both loudly shouting "Allah, Allah" in unison. Halfway down, the car noticeably slowed its descent and I looked at E. and said "Angels"!

Sure enough, the car gently descended after that, and we landed with a bounce well out into the fields below. I guess we had descended the equivalent of a four storey building. We were just fine . . . no shock, alert and thinking clearly.

On three wheels, we made our way out of there driving diagonally up a grassy slope until we reached the road above. Cars had pulled up, a crowd had gathered and the semi-trailer driver was pointing to the area where we took off into space. What a shock he got when our car slowly crawled out further down the road behind them! They made a big fuss of us and it was somehow joyful and moving. They didn't expect us to be alive, so perhaps the distance was greater than I remembered. (We didn't tell about the Angels).

One man kindly drove us to a small nearby town and told people about what had happened and how eerie it had been to see us appear back on the road when they thought we must be dead. He arranged for our tyre to be mended and drove us back to our car. While we waited in a coffee lounge, along came a Subud member whom E. had opened and who had drifted away. He was pleased to see us and joined us. As we parted, we promised to mail him a copy of Susila Budhi Dharma, which was what he requested.

From *Reminders of Reality*

THE SIGN

~ ANONYMOUS

Two young men from abroad were staying with me. One was a Subud member and the other one, his friend, wasn't. They were having lively discussions about the existence of God. The friend was an atheist and was challenging the Subud brother.

Two days later the friend went on holiday to Scandinavia while the other one went on to stay in my country. After about three weeks the friend came back and I invited both of them over. The Subud brother and I noticed that the friend was different since he had returned from his holiday. He was much more quiet and, frankly, seemed a bit shell-shocked. Later that day he shared with us what had happened during his holiday.

Before he'd left he had prayed and asked, 'God, if you exist, then give me a sign during this holiday.' One day he was driving his car in Denmark when he had a freak accident. During the accident he was flung out of his car in a most peculiar manner. The car ended up severely damaged. Had he stayed in it he wouldn't have survived the crash; as it was, he only had a few bruises.

Bystanders who had seen the accident happen, and later the police, spoke of a miracle and that they could not believe he had survived this accident; they all agreed that he should have been dead. He then thought about his prayer and had started to question his old belief system. That's why he had been so quiet and withdrawn.

I have lost touch with both of them since, but I am pretty sure that the friend who had the accident would not forget this experience for the rest of his life.

From *Reminders of Reality*

A New Experience for Bapak

It is necessary for Bapak to tell you a little about Bapak's recent experiences, while he was ill. Dr. Rachman took Bapak's pulse ~ he is a doctor who is close to Bapak, because he is a Subud member ~ and he found that Bapak's pulse rate was over a hundred-and-sixty. Rachman himself did not think it possible that Bapak would survive, because his pulse rate was so far above normal. Then they suddenly managed to discover a heart specialist, and this doctor was brought to Bapak's house. He also examined Bapak, and saw his condition. Bapak allowed himself to be examined. Indeed Bapak's illness was very, very dangerous, extraordinarily so, for the doctor said that the arteries were constricted. He examined Bapak with all the equipment he had brought with him. The heart was jumping about and beating irregularly. Eventually the doctor said that if Bapak would agree to this, he would like to put Bapak into hospital, where there would be more adequate equipment. Never before had Bapak said 'yes' to a doctor, but at that moment he said: "All right; take me to hospital."

'When will Bapak feel well enough to go there?'

'Take me there now.'

Bapak was taken to the hospital and thoroughly examined in the theatre there. The doctor at St. Carolus, a private doctor practicing at that Christian hospital, said that it would not be possible to cure Bapak with any ordinary equipment, and they left this to Bapak. Even then it would be a matter of chance. Bapak answered:

'Yes, human beings have no power over life and death. Life and death are in the hands of God. Bapak himself surrenders to God. You may carry out this treatment.'

It was carried out in the operating theatre by the doctors there. Eventually they succeeded. It did not all go quite right, but it went half right, though not all that well. And the assistants seemed to be very incompetent. When the cardiologist told them to do this and to do that, they made mistakes, but Bapak understood. They were being made stupid by the One Almighty God, so that they could follow the will of God being manifested in the human self. Then the instruments they were using soon went right and could resume their functioning, and eventually things went well and came out right, so that the doctor himself said to Bapak:

'I give thanks to Bapak and to the One Almighty God; Bapak has fortunately been able to recover from his illness.'

Bapak's pulse rate went down from hundred-and-sixty to seventy-two, so that the doctor himself was astonished, and he asked: 'What is all this, Bapak? Please explain to me what is Bapak's way.' I told him a little about Bapak's experience and also about what Bapak's function has been in human life, as Chairman of the Spiritual Brotherhood of Subud. The doctor was aware that Bapak's illness had been cured. 'Bapak must feel pleased', he said. But I did not feel pleased, for all that is from the power of the One Almighty God. I should feel just as pleased if in one hour's time God were to take Bapak's soul. That is why Bapak says that it is the One Almighty God.

Beginning from that moment, Bapak recovered from his exceptionally severe illness. The St. Carolus doctors themselves were astonished; someone who has gone through what Bapak experienced cannot normally survive it for more than twenty-four hours, while Bapak was able to endure it for six days and six nights, and his mind was still sound. I myself was astonished at the experience. This was a new experience for Bapak, brothers and sisters, so that for all of you it can bring you to understand it and weigh it up and to have faith that all of this was done by the One Almighty God. It was not the doctors who cured Bapak, it was no human being who cured Bapak, but the One Almighty God.

Bapak
Toronto, Canada, August 14, 1979

PREPARATIONS

IN DEATH

~ HALIMAH E. POLK

Many of us in my Subud generation are experiencing an upsurge in the deaths of beloved Subud brothers and sisters and family members. It's not totally unexpected since we are all aging, but still it can be confounding to hear almost weekly about the death of someone you loved or you knew. Fortunately, my own life in Subud has in some ways prepared me to confront death with an equanimity that sometimes mystifies my non-Subud friends and family.

It wasn't always like that. In my early years I listened to and read Bapak. What he told us about death was so different from my limited agnostic/secular point of view that his words never really registered and when they did register, set off a fearful cognitive dissonance. I obviously needed experience.

My first big death lesson came while I was living in Carmel Valley. One of our young members, Leonard Roberts (the son of Aisha Roberts) was killed in a car accident. The Carmel Valley Subud group was large and very active, but we were all bewildered. How could a son of such a stalwart Subud member living in Indonesia (who we felt had been entrusted to our care) die like this? In the midst of our preparations for a selamatan for Leonard, Aisha Roberts and her son Harris arrived at the Carmel Valley Subud House, having flown directly from Jakarta when they received the news. I remember so clearly Aisha sitting with all of us that beautiful May evening, reassuring us.

She had spoken to Pak Sudarto before she left and he told her that all was well. That some people only had to spend a short time here and when their work was completed they could return home. That Leonard was a special soul and it was his spirit that had led his mother to Subud, before he was even born on this earth. His mission on earth was fulfilled. Aisha was such an example for all of us, and especially for me as she was staying in my apartment during this time. She was able to exhibit such quiet grace in the midst of such an outward tragedy. Looking back, I am stupefied that a woman in the midst of what must have been excruciating grief could be so loving and giving to all of us. Her acceptance of death, the death of her own son, epitomized an approach to death that was unfathomable to me at the time

It was Aisha who said to me one night. "Halimah, why aren't you living in

Wisma Subud?" A question that changed my life forever. How did she know, I marveled, something I had forgotten, that Bapak had come to me a few years earlier in a dream and advised me to come to Indonesia to teach.

And, in fact, it was living in Indonesia for three years that really began to deconstruct my old head trips around death. The Indonesians and folks living at Wisma Subud were so unfazed by death; some even gleeful. I remember Hanafi Troncelliti remarking after the passing of one of the Indonesian helpers that he really liked it when someone passed away. "There was a special quiet in the air," he quipped. And of course all the selamatans and the careful observance of the rituals, washing the body, preparing the grave were all carefully proscribed and based, I discovered, on an awareness of spiritual principles totally foreign to me.

During my time in Indonesia, I had a dream that my Nana, my grandmother, was about to die. I took a month off from my teaching at the International school to fly home and spend time with her. My mother was caring for her in our home. Nana was quite relieved to see me, because she had been very distraught that I was living in Indonesia, such a far away and foreign country full of what she called "Mohammedans." When I told her how happy I was there she stopped fretting and was peaceful. During my stay I had the opportunity to spend many hours with her as she was approaching death. She was a very religious woman and was forever reassuring me that she was ready to go. But seemed most remarkable was how Nana would slip in and out of this world. Sometimes when I was sitting with her, I could feel my latihan start buzzing lightly; she was off in the next world for a few minutes, getting acquainted I guess. That "special quiet" when she would travel momentarily to the next world was palpable. I could feel it myself. Later after her death, I held the 1000 day selamatan in Indonesia for her with Bapak in attendance along with many Indonesian hadjis. (Muslim holy men, "those very Mohammedans" Nana had feared!).

About two years later when I had just returned to the USA from Indonesia, my brother Douglas died in a horrible car accident. This event was shattering and totally different from Nana's death – so much for spiritual principles! My family was devastated and everything seemed very murky, even nightmarish, about his death, because he had died in unsavory circumstances. There was no "special quiet" in the air (at least that I could feel.) Turning to the rituals I had absorbed while living in Indonesia, I was able to talk my mother into allowing me to host a selamatan in Miami where she lived and we invited a few friends and members of the local Subud group. I can remember watching my mother prepare for this selamatan and how simply preparing this special meal seemed to quiet both of us for a short while. When I returned to my home in San Diego, we observed several of the required selamatans for my brother as well, but still I was deeply shaken and in a dark place. By the grace of God, six months later I dreamt that I came into a room and saw my brother Doug lying on a sofa, just glowing and radiant. He was fine.

But the greatest lessons for me came with the death of my daughter, Mariama. Mariama was a severely handicapped child born with extensive brain damage and very limited mobility. She could cry, smile, turn her head, and hear music and voices, move her arms and legs just slightly. While Mariama was so damaged outwardly, she was physically beautiful and radiated a special something. In short she was a bundle of inner radiance and we were devoted to her. Because her brain damage was so dire, renowned specialists in Los Angeles had given her about a year to live, but Mariama, happily for us, lived until she was four and a half years old.

As you can imagine, my husband (at the time) and I were devastated by her death. Navigating such an intense emotional and spiritual cataclysm was only softened for me by visits from Mariama in dreams, in my latihans, and in actual life. I never saw her in the flesh but she often spoke to me —which she couldn't do while living. These visitations began to give a glimmer of what might be happening to Mariama in the next world. For one thing, in that world she was no longer trapped in an inhospitable body. Once while Sulfiati Magnuson and I were doing latihan during a very complicated surgery, I saw her leave her body and float way out into the ether. "Mom," she exclaimed, "I can sing. I can dance." In a dream after her 1000 day selamatan I found myself transported to the "other world" where they seemed to be having a celebration for Mariama simultaneous with ours here. In the dream, Mariama was sitting at the head of large conference table surrounded by older Subud members from Indonesia and around the world. During the "other world" celebration, Mariama got up on the table and took her first steps — something impossible for her while she was living. I wept with joy when I woke up from this dream.

Later on, Mariama came to tell me she how happy she was now as a student at a Catholic school over there. She had been baptized a Christian here so that seemed appropriate enough. She even asked for a more overtly Christian name to use at school so as to fit in more comfortably! Whatever…

As the years have passed since Mariama's death, indications suggest that Mariama has become a Subud helper working alongside many other souls on the other side to serve us here. It's not unusual that at large Subud gatherings at the opening latihan, I will sense her presence sitting right beside me. Once before leaving for a Subud National Congress in Vancouver, Washington, Mariama reported that she was going to be there as well. "We are going," she told me, "to hold the quiet."

When I went to Bapak's grave in 1989, Mariama's soul came as well to show her respects. In 1994 when I visited Bapak's new grave at Suka Mulia, Mariama came right to my side and sat quietly and loyally, even as Bapak bawled me out for mistakes I had made in my marriage. Once in the middle of a latihan at Menucha, Mariama asked my forgiveness for dying because she saw how difficult it had been for me. Of course, I was stunned. Truth be told I don't think I was harboring any ill feeling towards Mariama but even so to be asked... ah, a mother's dream. In an interview with Ibu Rahayu, she said, "Don't feel that your children (who have died) are no longer with you; they are with you all the time." At that moment she glanced past me and over my shoulder as if seeing a child by my side.

At one point I spoke to Ibu Rahayu about these visits from Mariama, because I was feeling guilty that perhaps Mariama's concern for me was holding her back from getting on with her new journey. No, Rahayu said it was a gift to me. So I am extremely grateful for these visits and lessons about life after death, lessons that have been an aspect of my Subud journey. It's as if when I am especially quiet, especially tuned in, a connection is made with this other hidden world... the world that was promised to us by Bapak in his talks and the world more clearly revealed to me by my own daughter Mariama after her death. I've taken great heart from these experiences, as should we all, despite periods of anguish and grief. And I know that many of us have had similar experiences with and visitations from loved ones who have passed away.

Death, for me, is definitely not the end; our development continues so we don't have to be finished with our purification or perfect at the time of death. We just sincerely do the best we can. What a relief! Moreover, there seems to exist an entire parallel universe "over there", gentler and lovelier, where we, together with loved ones, can continue to flourish in our love and work. Sometimes in latihan, I see my children and dear friends who have died just waiting expectantly for my coming home to them. And once I was allowed to feel in my heart the unspeakable joy of that reunion. Oh yes, I can still be very afraid of the process of dying, but I am, by God's grace, more fully at peace with death itself.

MR. SANDS

~ ANN PADILLA

Mr. Sands was 73. He wore all-white when he came to the clinic – white tennis shoes, white socks white painter's pants, white T-shirt and a white jacket. There was the pattern of a yardstick embedded on his cream-colored suspenders. He had been in the Navy and he always spoke as if he was still there. His wife was gone now and he had lung cancer.

"I am gonna die...Aye," he said. "I loved my wife and I love the sea. I don't have much to live for any more." He would ask, "How can I live while I am here?"... And "Will I be forgotten when I go?"

I was his palliative care provider. Over the course of the year, we formed a bond. He would talk, and I would listen. He would ask me how to live well while he was alive. He worried about being forgotten after he died.

He wanted people to remember him so he bought a big fishing license and often went to sea with his buddies. He caught every kind of big fish and would load ling cod and king salmon into a flat ice chest, prop it onto the handlebars of his walker and shuffle it into the clinic. He gave me a big fish to take home and told me to eat it.

"After I die, I want you to think of me every time you eat ling cod," he said. He made me promise I would eat it and remember him.

One day when he came to clinic I noticed his right arm was red, swollen and painful. "Aye," he said, "I had to go to the emergency room. I'm on antibiotics now. I'm on chemo so I got an infection."

"What happened?" I asked.

"I was riding the bus," he said, "I heard a man and woman arguing loudly. I saw him reel back and punch the woman in the face. The bus stopped and the man and woman got off. It was my stop so I got off too. The man continued to argue with the woman and suddenly, he punched her in the face again.

I thought of my mother. No man should strike a woman, for from the loins of a woman all life comes. I walked over to the man and thought I am weak and old and going to die. I reeled back and with all my might I punched the man to the ground. Someone in the crowd use their cell phone to call the police. An officer

came in and shouted me out. "I ought to throw you in jail," he said.
"Have at it," I told him.

And he wept.

Mr. Sands couldn't talk any more, so I talked to him as he cried.

"You don't care if you went to jail or got injured from hitting the man... Because you are going to stand up for what you believe in while you are here. You want to make a difference. You want to live before you go."

"Aye... You see me, not past me.... Aye," he said.

DRIVER TRAINING

~ AMELIA WILLIAMS

We are driving down an inclined road. There is a wide curve overlooking a long and deep vista. Gently we veer off the road, over the cliff and call "Allah!"

This was a re-occurring dream with Istiharoh Glasgow in the driver's seat and Olivia Panopoulos as side-kick navigator. I am in the back seat, and they are teaching me to die.

On one occasion there is another woman in the back seat with me. She feels like but not quite my mother, who is in an elder care facility preparing to pass on. Ahhh, I feel – this makes sense, in a dreamy sort of way. The next day I learn that my aunt, the sister to my 95 year old mom, has died.

I never shared these dreams with Isti or Olivia, who have left us now. But they showed me in their own last days that they knew how to die.

Sometimes when I am out running errands I am driving down an inclined road. There is a wide curve overlooking the sea. As I take the bend I smile....
"Allah!"

MY SENSES OF MY OWN DEATH

~ RICHARD SALISBURY

BACKSTORY

When I was 10, I went to the Berkeley (California) YMCA summer camp, Camp Gualala. I had a great time, playing tetherball, singing songs around the campfire, etc. One day a bus took my cabin-full of boys, and some others, winding down the mountainside to the beach. For part of the time we all (except maybe the camp counselors) went skinny-dipping in the Pacific Ocean. When it was near time to leave, the counselors invited us to have one last dip, the perfect end to one of the most fun days I can recall. The sun was just setting, and as I ran into the surf one more time, I filled with delight at the sensation of the cold, bracing water on my skin, and at the beauty of the sun, reflected on the water and turning the sky red. We dried off, dressed, and reboarded the bus. The mental picture of that final, ecstatic moment in the surf, a perfect blend of light, air, ocean, and feeling free, has never left me.

MAIN STORY

I was opened in Subud 12 years later – a lifetime it seemed then – soon after hearing of it from a college friend, Wayne Lerrigo.

I met my first wife at the 1971 Subud World Congress. We wed that fall, and moved to Santa Monica. A few months after our daughter's birth in fall 1972, I fell asleep on our sofa one evening, still dressed. I had a dream (dreams had already become a rich source of guidance for me):

I was an old black woman dying and alone in an isolated shack. I sat on a rickety chair at a rickety table. It was afternoon; tall trees dimmed the light coming through the doorway and window, and as the day became twilight then dusk, everything grew dark except for a lit candle on the table. She/I laid my head on my arms as I felt my life leaving. I sensed something outside me, darker than the complete darkness of the deep night: the absence of any presence other than myself, and the presence of an Absence. My sight dimmed; even the candlelight vanished in darkness. Alone and utterly terrified, I felt the Absence engulf me.

This is the only nightmare, or one of only two, that I believe I have ever had. If utterly terrifying to the old woman it was not to me, because even as I dreamed, my identification with her was not complete: I was also aware of being her observer.

I awoke at once and thought of my paternal grandmother, 88 years old and in a hospital north of San Francisco. Fearing she might be dying, I resolved to go to her. I scraped up money for a round trip airfare, and stayed with my aunt nearby for a day or two while I visited Grandmother. In our last visit I spoke to her about Subud for the only time. Among my family I'd made no secret of my involvement. But she had paid it little mind and now, though she listened politely, was plainly uninterested. She lived on another eight years, but died in a nursing home, mostly alone and, though outwardly a devout Christian, terrified of dying. So perhaps the dream did foretell her death. But many years later I suddenly knew that it was also, or primarily, about my death: the sort of death that, nine years in Subud, I unconsciously feared; and possibly the sort of death I would have had then.

Bapak died when I had been in Subud about 23 years. By then I had four children, and was in my second career (with one still to go).

I knew I would miss Bapak, would miss being in his presence and being guided and helped by his talks, by latihans with him, and most of all by his testing with us. I also wondered about the future of Subud without him. Still, I was not sad or worried. Soon after his death I had two experiences that I will call, with some hesitation, receivings. In one, I had a mental vision of the globe with points of light all over it, linked by lines of light, so the earth seemed as if girdled by a web of light. I thought this might foretell the growth of Subud or the growing influence of the latihan even after Bapak's death, though my worldly awareness of Subud gave my mind and heart little grounds for such optimism.

In the second receiving, I had a sudden mental picture of my death: I walked naked into the ocean just at sunset, as in that ecstatic moment 35 years before. I kept on till I was under water, the light growing dimmer and dimmer. In the same moment I realized that hitherto my sense of my death had been of being in complete darkness, alone. Now, walking willingly, freely, from fading sun into dark waters – when I thought about it after – did not strike me as ideal, or in line with what I had hoped for from reading and hearing Bapak. Yet in the moment, though tinged with sadness, it seemed more hopeful than just being lost in darkness, and carried with it no fear: rather, acceptance, openness, and some of the anticipation and awe I had felt when I was 10.

That same year, 1987, guided by the latihan, I decided to leave my second career, as a software technical writer, and become a psychotherapist – something I'd thought of since before being opened. A year later I started on an MA. Sometime in the '90s, still a new and struggling therapist, I had another unexpected mental vision. An inner voice told me that if I would continue to the end this work of helping others, then at the instant of death the Angels of Death would snatch me up. I thought of the African-American spiritual, "Swing Low, Sweet Chariot," but my vague mental picture was more as if two winged beings lifted me and flew away with me.

I suppose one could consider this vision and audition mere imagination, or consider the beings demonic. But, though a severe self-critic, I don't believe I've been so naughty that I need fear the latter. (At times I have feared it.) More to the point, what I felt was not dread but surprise, hope, and awe.

The last career, the longest of the three, has brought me much more inner growth than the first two. In the fall of 2013 I underwent a series of seemingly unconnected health crises, which, though not without danger, were shown by testing to be chiefly purification. I missed weeks of work, and with my wife's encouragement and the support of testing, decided to retire; I am more relaxed now, and quieter, inwardly and outwardly.

So the work I was guided to, and which I received would bring me to a better death, is done. And though any of us may die at any moment, the outer signs suggest I may live many years yet. So perhaps I still have before me the potential for more helping work. At any rate, I am more optimist than pessimist. I feel that I am not finished, and that God may yet will more work for me, maybe in an explicitly Subud context. My wife and I plan to attend the 2014 World Congress. I feel ready for anything – or for nothing special.

REST EASY

~ CESCA WRIGHT

I saw a photograph in the local *Davis Enterprise* of a group of women, sitting in a circle, singing to a person in the center. Immediately, I wanted to learn more.

They were members of the local Threshold Choir, practicing bedside singing. When I was in fifth grade, the nun who conducted the Sacred Heart Church Choir had told me to only open and close my mouth, but not to let sounds come forth. Except for *latihan*, I hadn't sung since. But the calling was strong. I mustered my courage, found where they met, and showed up. The songs were simple. The women were patient and kind. Even though I couldn't read music, I kept showing up and learning the songs.

Before long, I was invited to join others to sing, mostly to Hospice patients, at a local convalescent facility. We had a list of patients.

We came to a room that others had visited before. The patient was reclining, mouth open, eyes closed. Beside her was a middle aged woman reading a book. Against the wall were two teen girls, tapping their smart phones.

"We are the Threshold Singers, may we offer your family a song?" The woman looked uncertain. "We have been singing to Mrs. W for the past few weeks. Our music is non-denominational and is offered for pain relief and comfort. She has seemed to enjoy it." The woman closed her book and waved us in.

There were four of us at the foot of the bed. *"May you dwell in the heart, may you be free from suffering, may you be healed, may you be at peace."* We noticed that Mrs. W's breath was irregular. "Are you family members? May we offer you song as well? Please step closer to the bed and we'll stand behind you." The girls put down their phones and came closer to their grandmother. They took her hands and looked at her.

"In this moment, I open my heart. And receive all the love, that's always surrounding me..." the harmonies filled the room.

"Easy, rest easy. Let every trouble, drift away. Easy, rest easy, love enfolds you and holds you safe."

With those words, Mrs. W took her final breath, her daughter and granddaughters surrounding her. Tears began to flow. We quietly left.

(See ThresholdChoir.org for more about this ministry.)

THE CALL HOME

~ SERAFINA

I thought I was a soldier
Fighting the enemy
Standing as I had always stood
Ready to defend
This sparse and inhospitable territory

But the enemy came from within
Pounding the walls of my bloodline
with an unknown intruder
Flooding my veins
and a rough-shod heart
With a faultline going right through it.

The armour gone
I won't be a martyr
But an illusive dam buster
I am not ready to fall
I'm just so very tired.
All the time aware of movement within
The tingle up my spine
the presence in the room
which tells me you are there.

My feeling heart is tired of feeling
And the unknown intruder causes consternation
Knitted brows on the foreheads of men who
diagnose.
The intruder comes and goes and reappears
Like a bruised cloud moving across the sky
Changing shape accordingly.

Sometimes I feel like a still life
Waiting to metamorphose into a real painting.
I would like to be an illuminated manuscript
Not a post-it note fluttering mindlessly through the window of opportunity,
Relinquishing its hold on life.

At the pool, I repeatedly throw myself down the highest water slide
To feel alive again
Screaming with laughter
Sliding down into a baptism of my own making
I forget how bad I felt last week.

I feel like a fraud with
The emergency card
Tucked away in my purse
Nobody would guess
what is going on inside.
I am held in suspension
For my own good.

For, like most people I am not dying you see,
I am merely a potential candidate for the chop
It is only a matter of time.

Meanwhile, I acknowledge the presence of said intruder
biding its time
Its inconsistencies ruffling feathers
And try to befriend this wayward soul
Loitering on the edge of infinity

But I will not leave the room until my surrender is complete
For the call home
Is wide and born on wings of fire
This will not be my defeat.

LAST WISHES

~ MALAMA MACNEIL

when I die
gather in morning light
bring flutes and drums,
food, poems and prayers
share with one another
mention my name
sing "Simple Gifts"
and all the verses of "Amazing Grace"
hold one another
weeping while you laugh
remembering we came together
in times of levity as well as love
forgive my going so soon

linger all day at the edge of the sea
then walk into the hills I loved
watch for the circling birds of prey
I always thought I'd soar with them
given a choice
believe I've come to that
and to standing with the oldest tree
deep in the forest
to sighing with the wind
to sprouting up with rainborn winter grass
and to shining in the brazen light of a moon
pregnant with all we cannot know
in one brief life
gasp then or later
in delight at lying down
in the arms of those you hold most dear

and let your hearts break then
with remembering me
and how I loved life
not loud but deeply
not long enough but all the time
choose to live then
closer to the moment and more simply
smile the way I knew you best
bless each day, each place, each wondrous being
saying *now*, so be it, thank you
saying *yes*, even this
amen

December 6, 1994

Why the Latihan is Needed

For as Bapak often says about death and illness, it can be said that Bapak is speaking to you now and could die later. Now he is speaking, and tomorrow morning he could die. For death or illness we cannot control. We cannot get rid of an illness that is in us, nor can we avoid death. So, because we cannot avoid it but are sure to die, we very much need to know what death is, what there is in death. If, then, we already know what there is in death, we shall not waver, we shall not be distressed and feel bewildered by it. Death will just be death, because we already know about it, already understand it. That is what is necessary.

And that is why the Latihan Kejiwaan of Subud is needed. Thus the Latihan Kejiwaan is for us to be blessed by God, to be granted grace by God the Almighty, so that we can understand our situation after death or in death.

Bapak
Cilandak, Indonesia
March 28, 1976

I AM HOME

~ PAUL EDWARDS

Two days after his sudden death Hamid Camp came to me and we had this conversation:

Hamid: Hi Paul

Paul: Hi Hamid… we are very sad…

Hamid: I know…

Paul: No, the whole family is sad…

Hamid: I know…

Paul: The whole Subud group is sad… we are all sad…

Hamid: I know, I know, but I'm not…

Paul: How is it for you?

Hamid: You have no idea what it is like.

Hamid: I am swimming in an ocean of love…

Hamid: I am home…

An Overnight Stop

The messengers of God have already explained that conditions in the life after death are far wider and more glorious and more enduring than in this one.

In contrast our present life here in this world can be compared to an overnight stop or to someone on a journey who breaks it for one or two or three days, whereas afterwards, when you have left this world, the time is incomparably longer and can be called immeasurable.

Therefore pray to God that you will find your way there in your life after death, and that you will be able to work in that glorious world; a world far more glorious than this, the world that is truly heaven. Those of you who can already receive a little bit can catch a glimpse of that world.

Bapak
Cilandak, Indonesia
October 3, 1975

Made in the USA
Lexington, KY
13 January 2015